ROCKS,

DIRTY BIRDS,

AND BRIARS

ROCKS,

DIRTY BIRDS,

AND BRIARS

SOWING TRUTH IN A TIME OF LIES

FRANKLIN GRAHAM
and DONNA LEE TONEY

WORTHY*
Inspired

Published by Worthy Inspired, an imprint of Worthy Publishing Group, a division of Worthy Media, Inc.,
One Franklin Park, 6100 Tower Circle, Suite 210, Franklin, TN 37067.
WORTHY is a registered trademark of Worthy Media, Inc.

HELPING PEOPLE EXPERIENCE THE HEART OF GOD

eBook available at www.worthypublishing.com
Audio distributed through Oasis Audio; visit www.oasisaudio.com

Library of Congress Control Number: 2016941941

Quotation in the Introduction comes from Jewish Encyclopedia, s.v. "Sholem Asch," Polish-born, 1880–1957.

For foreign and subsidiary rights, contact rights@worthypublishing.com

ISBN: 978-1-61795-816-8 (second edition)

Cover Design: Melissa Reagan
Cover Images: istock.com

Printed in the United States of America
16 17 18 19 20 LBM 9 8 7 6 5 4 3 2

CONTENTS

ROCKS,

DIRTY BIRDS,

AND BRIARS

FOREWORD

J esus Christ is the outstanding personality of all time," wrote Sholem Asch, Yiddish author and playwright. "In all history, both as Son of God and Son of Man . . . no other teacher—Jewish, Christian, Buddhist, Mohammedan—is still a teacher whose teaching is such a guidepost for the world we live in. Other teachers may have something basic for an Oriental, an Arab, or the Occidental; but every act and word of Jesus has value for all of us. Everything he ever said or did has value for us today and that is something you can say of no other man, dead or alive. There is no easy middle ground to stroll upon. You either accept Jesus or reject him."

While there is no evidence that this famed author was a follower of Jesus Christ, he certainly believed that Jesus was *who He claimed to be*—and there can be no better setting for the parable of the sower told by Jesus

Himself. Scripture says, "Every word of God is flawless" (Proverbs 30:5 NIV).

As Jesus walked the sandy shores of the fishing village with His disciples, it was common for large crowds to gather and follow after Him to hear His words. Some were curious. Some were skeptical. Some were burdened. Some were joyous.

The words of Jesus *challenged* inquiring minds.

His words *convicted* critical spirits.

His words *comforted* weary hearts.

His words *captivated* those who loved Him.

This is the Son of Man as the *Preacher, Teacher*, and *Friend*. This is Jesus sowing the seed of truth into stony hearts and thirsty souls. Perhaps you can picture people gathering as Jesus climbed into a boat and sat looking into faces that had been fashioned by His hands.

His lips longed to speak truth to hearts that were hostile and hearts that were humble.

His eyes peered into souls for which He would soon give His very life to die in their place.

As the waters of Galilee lapped against the boat

and the lake breeze brushed across His face, the people standing at the water's edge eagerly listened as the wise Teacher said . . .

"And *a sower* went out to sow . . ." (Mark 4:3 ESV).

Jesus used the parables, and especially the parable of the sower, to teach us many things, and as with all inspired Scripture, God's Word speaks directly into people's lives in very specific ways to help us distinguish truth from lies.

The lessons gleaned from the parables of Jesus are innumerable. Some say He spoke in riddles, but every word He spoke was truth. His truth overshadowed philosophers. His truth underscored Himself (John 1:1).

Jesus laid aside His glory to walk among men.

His steps carried Him across the plains and hillsides proclaiming forgiveness and salvation for mankind. He sowed good seed in repentant hearts.

His steps carried Him to Calvary, where He laid down His life to save the human race from sin that leads to eternal separation from almighty God. Even in death, He sowed seed that reestablished a relationship between God and man. There, the Rejected One became the Thorn-Bearer as He endured Satan's snares and the crown of thorns placed upon Him by his captors.

But the Seed that died was resurrected, and Christ stepped from the Garden Tomb on Easter morning vacating a grave that could not hold the Savior of the world.

And we are told in Scripture to "follow in His steps" (1 Peter 2:21).

Jesus identifies Himself as the Sower of good seed (Matthew 13:37). He set the example of what He desires His followers to do: Proclaim the Word of God, the Gospel of Christ.

There have been countless believers who have obediently followed His command: "Go into all the world and preach the gospel" (Mark 16:15).

I am grateful that my father, Billy Graham, has been among those who have scattered the good seed of God's Word from city to city, country to country, and continent to continent, following in the steps of Jesus. He often says, "Evangelism is not a calling reserved exclusively for the clergy. I believe the greatest priority of the church today is to mobilize all followers of Christ to do His work. Those who do the work of sowing the seed know that much inevitably falls upon stony ground that bears no fruit, but if only a few seeds flourish, the results are manifold."

Many may not realize that my father sowed seed as a farm boy in Charlotte, North Carolina. There is no question that the Lord implanted his heritage deep into fertile soil.

As a young man he learned the principles of sowing and planting. When God called him to preach the Gospel, he applied what he had learned early in life—preparing, planting, and harvesting. These have served as the blueprint for ministry: prepare the soil in prayer, plant the seed of the Gospel by faith, and harvest souls for God's kingdom.

This is my purpose for encouraging people of faith to sow seed through prayer and action. We must pray for revival in the church. We must be proactive in working to turn our nation back to God by praying for, and supporting, those who will seek leadership roles in our schools, communities, and government—standing for the biblical principles that made our nation strong and blessed by the Lord.

Never before have I seen such a sharp rift in the moral and spiritual fabric of our country. The cross of

Christ is the dividing line between the righteous and the unrighteous, between the deceitfully dark powers of evil and the liberating light of the Gospel, between the virtues of godly living and the unfettered lusts of corrupt, debased passions. The wisdom and power of the cross appear as foolishness to those who suppress the truth and rebel against its claims. We are a people and a nation in imminent danger.

In the secular age, the influence of biblical principles and values has a diminishing impact upon education, government, and politics. Christians are not just simply tolerated—we are under constant, unrelenting assault for our beliefs and practices. "America the Beautiful" is under assault by rocks of political correctness, by dirty birds that feed on immorality, and by the briars that are choking the very life out of a nation that once proclaimed "In God we trust." Washington and our political system are fractured. We've seen violence at political rallies. One candidate is under investigation by the FBI. Another candidate says we need a political revolution. One thing I'm sure of—what America really needs is a spiritual transformation from the godless to the godly!

It will only happen if we turn back to God, who offers true freedom. The urgent need for our nation is obvious: to humble ourselves before Him with repentance and through prayer, asking Him to intervene for His glory and honor.

This has been the focus of my Decision America Tour, going across the nation, to all fifty states, to lead prayer rallies on the Capitol steps. Our nation is broken—politically, morally, and spiritually. Only almighty God can heal our nation—but it starts in the individual heart—welcoming the seed of Gospel truth, repenting of sin with hearts willing to be transformed, and embracing the whole truth and then resolving to make biblical principles the deciding factor by voting to restore the moral fiber of our nation. We must pray fervently that God will turn our nation back to Him who blessed it in the first place.

I have been asked many times if my father would be involved in calling the church and a nation back to God through such a program as Decision America. My friend, if my father were my age today, he would be leading it. While declining health and old age have silenced his powerful voice, his prayers are not silenced.

I trust that this book will be a tool in your hands to help you realize your own potential for sowing the seed of truth wherever your footsteps take you. The story that follows will tap your reserves and put your feet in motion as you step out of your comfort zone and into the fields of harvest, for the time is coming when Christ Himself will step down from the clouds of glory for the great harvest gathering. The task is not confined to preachers and missionaries. We can all be sowers of the Gospel truth even in a time of lies.

God bless you as you put your hand to the plow as a faithful sower and follow in the steps of the Sower.

Franklin Graham
Boone, North Carolina
April 2016

INTRODUCTION

A n all-out frenzy at the turn of the century was called
Y2K. The entire world was terrorized by the idea
that it would crash and burn as the clock struck midnight
on New Year's Eve. Some airlines parked their fleet on
December 31, 1999, in fear that if planes took flight
they could drop from the air. People huddled around
televisions that scrolled speculations, fueling fears. News
anchors spoke of potential catastrophic devastation.

The growing alarm was over two little numbers, 00.
Doubt mounted as to whether existing computers could
distinguish between 1900, the start of the twentieth
century, and 2000 marking the beginning of the twenty-
first century. (Computer data had been programmed to
use only the last two digits of the year.) Fear escalated, as
people believed that a little glitch in cyberspace would
confuse the centuries. Global doomsday fears mounted.

Worldwide businesses, industries, and governments

had been convinced that existing technology could not decipher the difference. The solution? Dump millions of computers and replace them with the latest and greatest before the new century arrived.

JUST A GLITCH

As the nations watched with bated breath, eyes were transfixed on the outlying islands in the Pacific Ocean, the first that would see the dawn of the third millennium. A frantic population, which had just celebrated the biggest holiday of all by watching *How the Grinch Stole Christmas,* shook in its boots thinking that the world was coming to an end.

But the *ringing in* reverberated well into the morning hours with billowing sighs of relief, and then with explosive celebrations—the world had not blown up! And the *Glitch did not steal the New Year,* as evidenced by the "antiquated" computers that easily made the leap into another day, another dollar.

The biggest news flash was not the fireworks that went off on January 1, but the tech stock that skyrocketed in the early days of the new millennium, eventually causing the bubble to burst. Nations watched the economic decline bulldoze hopes and dreams. Called the "hoax of the millennium," an online article posted, "Since the Internet has made instant communication possible between the furthest reaches of the globe, rumors and innuendo have spread faster than a sneeze on a crowded bus." A story that affected the entire world seemed to set the stage for the twenty-first century to fast become known as the Era of Fraud.

JUST A GAME

So it shouldn't come as a surprise that contrasting "truth and lies" has become a wildly popular pastime used for cultivating comradery.

"Two Truths and a Lie." It's a game.

It's used as an "ice breaker" for effective team-building.

It helps people get to know one another, social media claims.

Not only have we grown accustomed to the high-tech world being terrorized, we are growing accustomed to the indistinguishable. The rules of engagement for this game are straightforward. One person lists three "facts" about themselves, except one of the "facts" is a lie, and the other players have to guess which fact is "the lie." Let's stop right there. One of the *facts* is a lie? How does that work? In the late twentieth century, a politician was once asked if he was telling the truth or lying. He said: "It depends on what the meaning of 'is' is." Changing the meaning of a word "is" deceptive—deception is a lie. (Deception means "the act of making someone believe something is true when it is not.")

The dictionary plainly states that a fact is "a true piece of information." The dictionary also states that a lie is "a false statement or action with the intent to deceive."

Sadly, the human race is deceitful. Devouring one another with rapid fire on live television has become a devious sport; people calling others liars whether it is true or not. While Western civilization gasps at the reality that people in the Middle East are still stoned to death, people who claim to be civilized gleefully cast accusing stones at others with opposing views and then brag about the art of competition.

But our purpose is not to debate why people prey on lies. Our intent is to reveal why the spirit of mankind hides from the truth: because the heart of man is wicked. This is nothing new, but because of instant communication and a twenty-four-hour news cycle, society feeds on anything and everything that happens with more frequency than eating three meals a day. And when people feed on lies, it brings out the worst in the human spirit and causes societal behavior to go from bad to worse. What kind of example is this for our children and grandchildren, who seldom see truth as virtue and the standard by which to live their lives?

We live in a rocky world that can keep us off balance. While the center of earth has as its foundation a massive rock formation, a small, insignificant pebble trapped inside a shoe can cause tremendous pain with each step. Lies, big or little, have the same effect. Because we live in a world stained with sin, Satan plants his evil works into every facet of earthly life. It may start off insignificant, but that little pebble can become like a destructive boulder.

JUST LIKE GOD

Remember the original lie? The lie of all lies sprung up in the fertile and beautiful Garden of Eden. In Satan's pride, he disguised himself in the form of a serpent slithering onto the scene, perhaps through a jeweled rock formation. There, he planted the seed of doubt in Eve's heart that God was holding something back from the first couple—robbing them of His very best. She took the bait, trading God's truth for a lie as she reached up into God's bountiful harvest and plucked the forbidden fruit. Then she passed it on to Adam. From that moment in time, sin has been passed on. As the first couple bit into the fruit from the vine, the bitterness of sin took root in their hearts. This is Satan's game—he convinced Eve to exchange two truths for a lie.

God said to Adam, "Of every tree of the garden you may freely eat; but of the tree of the knowledge of good and evil you shall not eat, for in the day that you eat of it you shall surely die" (Genesis 2:16–17). But the serpent lied to Eve, "You will not surely die. For God knows that the day you eat of it your eyes will be opened, and you will be like God" (Genesis 3:4–5). From that moment, mankind has been twisted in the briars of Satan's lies.

To learn about lies that devour and the truth that cleanses, we turn to the Bible. This is where truth and lies are defined. There is "the God of truth" (Isaiah 65:16) and the devil, who has always hated the truth, because "there is no truth in him . . . for he is a liar and father of it" (John 8:44). Here we see Satan's intent to sow discord—lies—in the heart of every individual . . . and *we the people* often and gladly do his dirty work by engaging in it, or cheering it on.

JUST THE GOSPEL

This brings us to the Parable of the Sower, as told by Jesus Himself. As Jesus sat in the boat on Galilee and began telling His story, perhaps He thought about the "seed of the lie" planted in Eden. So, He who is the Truth painted the picture of a plowed field, prepared and ready to receive good seed. He described the fertile field and told of the patches of rocky soil where the sun scorched the seed. When the wind blew seed into matted vines, the twisted briars choked them out. Other seeds fell into shallow ground, taking root enough to produce sprouts. Then along came the dirty birds swooping down into the rocks and briars, stealing away the seed. Who are those dirty birds? ***The enemy of the harvest.***

There is a luminous cloud that hovers over lost souls. Sin, implanted by Satan, the great deceiver, darkens their hearts. But when the seed of truth is scattered, some grab hold until they listen to Satan tell them, *God's Word is a lie.* He causes them to doubt, and they let go of the truth. The danger in listening to Satan's lie is that it flourishes in human hearts, causing people to resemble Satan and mock God through their words and deeds. Today we see an unprecedented display of lies pitting neighbor against neighbor and citizen against citizen. So much for being one nation under God.

News headlines reveal that many people from all walks of life are cynical about the truth. They shrug their shoulders at lies. Religion is also a hot topic that has driven the media to dig for answers to the question, "Who is really a Christian?" The answer is hard for many—even those who claim the Christian faith. But it has opened up a worthy discussion and driven people to the Bible.

Here is what God's Word says, "You know the difference between truth and lies. And who is a liar? Anyone who says that Jesus is not the Christ" (1 John 2:20–22 NLT). "For the Spirit teaches you everything you need to know, and what he teaches is true—it is not a lie." (1 John 2:27 NLT). "Those who have been born into God's family do not make a practice of sinning, because God's life is in them. . . . So now we can tell who are children of God and who are children of the devil. Anyone who does not live righteously . . . does not belong to God" (1 John 3:9–10 NLT).

The Bible says that Satan is "the prince of the power of the air" (Ephesians 2:2), and we can certainly see the manifestation of this today in the messaging that dominates the airwaves.

Largely because technology has connected people to one another with a tap or click on a mobile device, the seeds of accusations are flung into cyberspace and tweets mount up quickly before anyone can determine whether they are truth or fiction.

The only search engine that can bring clarity to the "truth versus lie" debate is God's Word. He has given us the engine of truth, not to browse, but to study. Its power is demonstrated in clarifying fact versus fiction. So as we consider rocks that break us, dirty birds that hover over us, and briars that entangle, let's consider the following facts.

Rocks over the course of time can transform from one type into another. Rocks can represent strength, as in building a house upon the rock; or they can be used in the hands of cowards who get a kick out of throwing them at others. The latter is the picture of Satan, who transforms himself into an angel of light, persuading others to carry out his evil deeds. He embeds his hatefulness into the hearts of mankind, all too anxious to do harm. The Bible says, "For Satan himself transforms himself into an angel of light to do the work of iniquity" (2 Corinthians 11:14).

Dirty Birds are buzzards and vultures, thieves and predators up to no good. They swoop in to steal seed that a hardworking farmer has planted. These birds of prey also feed on dead carcasses. Satan is a dirty old bird when he plucks seeds of truth from human hearts that are dying in sin. The Bible also describes him as a roaring lion and warns, "Be of sober spirit, be on the alert. Your adversary, the devil, prowls around like a roaring lion, seeking someone to devour" (1 Peter 5:8 NASB). "Wherever the corpse is, there the vultures will gather" (Matthew 24:28 NASB).

Briars are a mass of thorns and prickly stems twisted like a network of wires. They are a barrier to the rain, a thorny trap that rips open flesh, leaving the sting of horror and scars that don't heal. They are good for nothing! "But if a field bears thorns and thistles, it is useless.

The farmer will soon condemn that field and burn it" (Hebrews 6:8 NLT).

The biggest lie that Satan plants in the human heart is that God's Word is not truth. He is going to do everything in his satanic power to scorch out, choke out, and steal away God's truth. But the "fact" is absolute: God's Word is unchangeable and infallible. God's Word is Truth. God's Word is the Gospel Seed that produces truthfulness, holiness, and obedience—and we are called to plant it.

Rocks may be thrown at you—duck!

Dirty birds may try to steal it away from your heart—hang on!

Briars may attempt to choke its power—keep planting, for God's truth will stand.

God's people are called to ***sow truth in a time of lies.*** So let's listen from the shores of Galilee as Jesus steps into the boat. . . .

JESUS
THE SEA MASTER

And again [Jesus] began to teach by the sea. And a great multitude was gathered to Him, so that He got into a boat and sat in it on the sea, and the whole multitude was on the land facing the sea.

Mark 4:1

In the Gospels, Jesus is often described as being near the sea. Jesus sat by the sea, walked on the sea, sent unclean spirits into the sea, traveled by sea, and withdrew from great crowds to the sea.

This is where we find Jesus when He told the parable of the sower, the seed, and the soils. Interestingly, He chose the sea as the backdrop to teach about sowing seed. Perhaps it was an unspoken message to the crowd that not even deep waters should prevent us from sowing the seed of the Gospel. Jesus sowed the seed of faith in Peter when the disciples saw Jesus walking on the water during a storm on the sea. They learned from the Miracle Maker that faith conquers fear. When Jesus later told them the parable of the mustard seed (a small seed), he said, "If you have faith as a mustard seed, you can say to this mulberry tree,

> Not even deep waters should prevent us from sowing the seed of the Gospel.

'Be pulled up by the roots and be planted in the sea,' and it would obey you" (Luke 17:6). Jesus was sowing faith, not fear. "Therefore with joy you will draw water from the wells of salvation" (Isaiah 12:3).

While the multitude marveled at Jesus' story, they could not comprehend it. Jesus told His disciples that unless they understood the parable of the sower, they would likely not understand the other parables (Mark 4:13).

The portrait Jesus paints with words in this parable identifies a sower, the seed, and the soils. The Bible says, "Blessed are you who sow beside all waters" (Isaiah 32:20).

> Scripture teaches that we reap
> what we sow, and in that sense
> we are all sowers.
> What kind of sower are you?

We are what we think. Thoughts become words. Words become actions. Actions become deeds. Actions breed good or evil. The billows in life's sea push us into the pathway of others who watch our lives and listen to our words, just as we observe others. Everything our minds soak up and every word that flows from our lips makes some impact, whether good, bad, or indifferent. When the waves smack us with fear because of doubt or the lies of deception, do we falter in the tumult of the deep waters, or do we keep walking toward Jesus in faith? Sowing the seeds of faith will conquer fear in tumultuous times and just may encourage others who are watching to exchange their fear for faith in **Jesus, the Sea Master.**

> *He will be a vessel for honor, sanctified and useful for the Master, prepared for every good work.*
>
> *2 Timothy 2:21*

JESUS
THE TEACHER

Then [Jesus] taught them many things by parables, and said to them in His teaching. . . .

As we read God's Word, we are inspired by Jesus revealing the heart of His Father in heaven. Jesus was sent to earth to die for the sins of mankind, yet in the Father's compassion and mercy for man's ignorance of God's love, He also sent His Son to walk among His creation—on land and sea—teaching truths that shed light upon darkened souls. Here at the sea, Jesus looked into sin-sick souls that thirsted for living water and eternal life, but the people could not comprehend the overwhelming love of God. Patiently He taught them. "I will open My mouth in parables; I will utter things kept secret from the foundation of the world" (Matthew 13:35).

Many wonder why Jesus taught using parables. Among the roles Jesus filled while on earth was schoolmaster. He encountered those who did not believe He was the Christ, but still called Him "Teacher" (Luke 18:18). And Jesus called even His disciples "children" (John 21:5).

How often do schoolteachers stand before their classes and tell stories as a way to illustrate the lesson? They don't simply ask, "What is ten minus two?" Instead, they draw a picture so that the children can visualize the question. "Johnny picked ten delicious red apples from the tree and then ate two of them. How many are left?" You can just imagine a child holding up ten little fingers and bending two of them down, then carefully counting eight fingers.

Jesus understood the learning style of His listeners, and He spoke to them accordingly. He painted pictures with words. As He walked the countryside, He taught His disciples about what was to come. "Nevertheless I tell you the truth. It is to your advantage that I go away; for if I do not go away, the Helper will not come to you; but if I depart, I will send Him to you. . . . For the Holy Spirit will teach you" (John 16:7; Luke 12:12).

What is the Holy Spirit teaching
you through the parables
of Jesus in His Word?

Ignoring the Lord's presence is dangerous! And we fall short of learning what He wants to teach us because, often, we are listening to the *wrong* voice. Peter certainly "fell short" in the waters of Galilee. He forgot momentarily the truth Jesus revealed—that He was the Way of safety; that Jesus Himself was the Source of miracles. Perhaps Peter heard "another" voice that planted a seed of doubt, or perhaps Peter became self-

> Jesus understood the learning style of His listeners, and He spoke to them accordingly.

aware that "he" was walking on water, thinking it was by his own power. Regardless, Peter took his eyes off of Jesus. As long as Peter walked toward the Lord on the water in faith, he learned that faith overcomes fear, but when Peter looked *down*—just for a moment—he faltered.

Because God is for us, He sent the Holy Spirit to reside in those who believe. We can walk to Jesus, and with Jesus, through the presence of His Spirit. Obeying Him is possible when our eyes are fixed on the Lord. He tills the soil of our hearts with the understanding of His ways, bringing clarity and application to His truth.

The Bible says, "For indeed I am for you, and I will turn to you, and you shall be tilled and sown"

(Ezekiel 36:9). The Holy Spirit sows in us the assurance that He will never leave us or forsake us. When Jesus ascended to His Father, He fulfilled His promise to send the Holy Spirit to help us distinguish truth from lies, faith from fear. Instruction comes from the Spirit of God and is exemplified by **Jesus, the Teacher**.

[Jesus,] the Teacher has come and is calling for you.

John 11:28

JESUS
THE SOWER

Listen! Behold, a sower went out to sow. . . .

Mark 4:3

Jesus often identified Himself with farmers. Farming is the first vocation for man the Lord established when He created Adam. He told Adam that he would toil over the land that would produce herbs and thorns— good and bad (Genesis 3:17–18) and the bad came as a result of sin. When Jesus came into the world, He took upon Himself the form of a servant (Philippians 2:7) and sowed good seed in the soil of souls to root out sin that steals away the joy of serving Him.

In the parable of the wheat and tares (Matthew 13:36–43), Jesus identifies Himself as the Sower. His disciples said, "Explain to us the parable of the tares" (Matthew 13:36). Jesus answered, "He who sows the good seed is the Son of Man. The field is the world, the good seeds are the sons of the kingdom, but the tares [the bad seeds] are the sons of the wicked one. The enemy who sowed them [the tares] is the devil, the harvest is the end of the age, and the reapers are the angels" (Matthew 13:37–39).

Because of Adam and Eve's sin (disobeying God in the Garden), Satan spoiled the perfection of man's life on earth and he has been sowing seeds of wickedness ever since. Jesus cautioned His followers to beware of those who sow bad seed (Satan's lies) and warned, "You will know them by their fruits. Do men gather grapes from thornbushes or figs from thistles? Even so, every good tree bears good fruit, but a bad tree bears bad fruit . . . every tree that does not bear good fruit is cut down and thrown into the fire. Therefore, by their fruits you will know them" (Matthew 7:16–20).

The Bible tells us that we are to pray for discernment. When we listen to others, we must study God's Word to see if what we are hearing is grounded in truth. Likewise, we must carefully examine that what we say and do exemplifies the truth of Scripture. We must pray for the Lord's discernment in our relationships and in our step-by-step walk with God. It is only through His enlightenment that we can recognize the fruit that reveals His nature.

Is the good seed of the Gospel being sown into and nourished in your heart so that you can recognize good from evil, truth from lies?

Seeds of wickedness thrive from ancient days. Its manifestation is seen at every turn. People excuse bad behavior because they believe there are no consequences. We are living in a time when lying is exalted by saying it doesn't matter. Political polls reveal that some candidates lie about their past and voters elect them to office anyway. We read about people who lie on job applications to get the job. People spread lies about others to make themselves look good, completely ignoring that God said, "Be sure your sin will find you out!" (Numbers 32:23). Without daily guidance of the Spirit, human hearts cannot discern good from evil.

The Bible tells us "A false witness who speaks lies [is], one who sows discord" (Proverbs 6:19). Our culture feeds on lies, but Christ's

> Satan spoiled the perfection of man's life on earth and he has been sowing seeds of wickedness ever since.

church is called to feed on truth—to sow truth in a time of lies. Satan does all within his power to steal the seed of God's truth. Simply put, consequences follow. When truth is absent, lies mount on deceptive wings and take to the air.

The apostle wrote to believers not to be "carried about with every wind of doctrine, by the trickery of men, in the cunning craftiness of deceitful plotting" but rather speak "the truth in love" and "grow up in all things into . . . Christ" (Ephesians 4:14–15).

The nations of the world are in search of truth. Let's faithfully proclaim it and stand on it. Truth will penetrate our souls if we feed on God's Word and let it take root in our hearts, planted by **Jesus, the Sower.**

The Lord GOD will cause righteousness and praise to sprout forth before all the nations.

Isaiah 61:11

JESUS
THE SOURCE

And it happened, as he sowed, that some seed fell by the wayside; and the birds of the air came and devoured it.

Mark 4:4

When building their nests, birds fly on a scavenger hunt for twigs, clods of mud, and wet, leafy compresses. They swoop into tree branches to set up house for a season and scout out the landscape to find seeds for themselves and worms for their young. Jesus uses birds throughout Scripture to teach lessons and give illustrations about His truth, for the Lord feeds the fowl of the air and tells us that we are more valuable to Him than the birds He watches over (Matthew 6:26).

Preparation of the soil is important to one who invests in seed with the hope of producing a bountiful harvest. A sower is careful about the art of sowing and planting in good soil, but a sower cannot control the wind that sweeps away scattered seed. A sower cannot stop rain from gushing through a freshly plowed field, dislodging a day's labor. Nor can a farmer shoo birds away from eating his freshly planted crop.

There are many principles and methods for sowing seed. Some seeds need to be buried in the ground; other seed can be scattered and still take root. Yet ravens, crows, and vultures have keen radar and prey upon a farmer's toil, pilfering seeds wherever they land. While God can use a raven as an agent of good, as in the case of the ravens feeding Elijah (1 Kings 17:4), Satan can use such a bird as an agent of evil. In this case, we see the birds of the air snatching away the seed of the Gospel.

This is the picture Jesus gives us in the parable. The "sower went out to sow . . . [but] some seed fell by the wayside," ground that had been trampled by foot and was too hardened for the seed to grow (Luke 8:5), so the dirty birds snatched up the seed. The seed that feeds the birds will never take root to produce a bountiful harvest.

> When the seed of the Gospel
> falls upon the soil of your soul,
> do you let it feed the birds,
> or are you nourishing it
> with the things of God?

Feed, seed, and everything you need was a slogan tacked up on a clapboard supply store in a small farming community. This verse came to mind: "God shall supply all your need according to His riches in glory"

(Philippians 4:19). The farmer plants seed and hopes for rain to water his crop. When rain does not come, he prays for it, knowing that God supplies the seed and the feed, and fulfills the needs according to His will. The Bible says, "[God] who supplies seed to the sower and bread for food will supply and multiply your seed for sowing and increase the harvest of your righteousness" (2 Corinthians 9:10 NASB).

> While God can use a raven as an agent of good, Satan can use such a bird as an agent of evil.

Satan, though, is the great deceiver, and if we are not careful to recognize the Source of the seed, we can easily become distracted and not pay attention to where the seed is planted. The dirty birds—Satan's minions—do their evil deeds in the unprepared soil of the human heart. We fail to nourish the seed of truth with the Water of life and the seed is snatched away, preventing the roots from taking hold. The Bible says, "The seed shrivels under the clods" (Joel 1:17). The seed of the Gospel truth is provided and we are responsible to spread it wherever we go, nourishing it with prayer. For Jesus is not only our example, **Jesus is the Source.**

> [The LORD] will give rain for the seed with which you sow the ground, and bread, the produce of the ground, which will be rich and plenteous.
>
> Isaiah 30:23 ESV

JESUS
THE LIVING STONE

Some [seed] fell on stony ground, where it did not have much earth; and immediately it sprang up because it had no depth of earth.

Mark 4:5

The Bible makes many references to stones. There were stone tablets for law-giving and stone altars for worship, engraved stones for memorializing and smooth stones for slaying a giant. There were stone foundations for kings' palaces and a stone that sealed the tomb of the King of kings . . . but only for a brief time.

There were stones that caused the foot to stumble and the Cornerstone that secured our foundation. There were mill-stones of violence and stones surrounding the throne of the Prince of Peace. There were stones of death and the living stones mentioned in 1 Peter 2:5.

Stones absorb water, so when seed falls into stony ground, it is robbed of moisture and has little soil in which to take root. This is what happens to the Seed of Truth— the Word of God— when it falls into stony hearts.

But here in the parable of the sower, Jesus describes seed that falls on ground that has been strewn with stones. Stones absorb water, so when seed falls into stony ground, it is robbed of moisture and has little soil in which to take root. This is what happens to the Seed of Truth—the Word of God—when it falls into stony hearts. The Bible says that we are to feed upon the Word of God (Job 23:12). While we are sowing the Gospel where our feet carry us, we should pray that the seed will fall on fertile ground—ground that has been plowed by prayer for the lost. Jesus said that if we are silent in our witness of Him, the very stones will cry out and proclaim His salvation (Luke 19:40).

Are you praying that the power of God would both soften the soil of your heart and water your prayers with tears of compassion for dry and hardened hearts that need to be tenderized?

Is it really just a childish phrase? "Sticks and stones may break my bones, but names will never hurt me." If hearts are pliable, they hurt. Hurting hearts are often filled with fertile soil. Hearts can be mended. Calloused hearts, however, often do not sense hurt; in fact, calloused hearts often go the extra mile to harm others.

These grim bearers of harshness can weaken believers and cause others to crack while walking through life's stony patches.

Troubled times will either soften us or cause rebellion to set in. The remedy is to refuse entrance to the unwelcome caller; don't even listen to the knock on the door. Instead, crack open the Bible and saturate your mind with the things of God. The Word of Truth will humble us and focus our attention on Almighty God. His power brings conviction to the heart. His prodding brings confession to the sinner. The Lord brings comfort to wounded spirits. Scripture tells us that "He who hardens his heart will fall into calamity" (Proverbs 28:14). When our hearts are cold and stony toward the things of God, it reveals that we have opened our heart's door to Satan. Why should we even give him a stepping-stone into our lives? "Do not sin," the Bible says, "nor give place to the devil" (Ephesians 4:26–27). The only way we can make room for Christ is to sweep sin out the back door so that He can come in through the front door and abide there. Make room in your transformed heart for **Jesus, the Living Stone.**

> *He is the Rock, His work is perfect; for all His ways are justice, a God of truth . . . righteous and upright is He.*
>
> *Deuteronomy 32:4*

JESUS
THE WATCHTOWER

But when the sun was up [the seed] was scorched, and because it had no root it withered away.

Mark 4:6

The Lord watches what we do with what He has given. In the parable of the talents (Matthew 25:14–30), Jesus described how a master gave three servants different values of talents (a form of money) and trusted they would use them wisely. The first two wisely increased what they had been given for the master. The last servant did nothing with what he was given except to hide it in the ground. When the master returned, the last servant excused his laziness by claiming he had protected it out of fear of the master. The master rebuked the lazy servant for his untruthful representation, claiming that he reaped where he had not sown and had gathered where he had not scattered seed.

Here is the picture of seed that had nothing to draw from, burned up by the heat of the day. Imagine opening a bag of fresh sunflower seeds and scattering them on parched ground. Unless they are confiscated by wildlife, the seeds will dry up and be blown away by the wind.

Many listening to the story had no understanding. They could not grasp the lessons Jesus was teaching about the sower, seed, and soils. At times we don't even realize where we are sowing the seed of the Gospel. Perhaps we've talked to a family member, neighbor, or fellow worker about what God has done in our lives, but they do not take it to heart. The good seed we sow lands on dry ground. Time passes and we forget about their dehydrated souls. The world's system has drained their hearts of spiritual nutrients. Or perhaps they offend us and we retaliate in a harsh way. We use careless words to satisfy our position. Sometimes our testimony is scorched by human anger instead of demonstrating God's spirit of forgiveness. We are to exemplify Christ living in us every moment of every day. You may say, "That is impossible!" But it isn't impossible if we remember *who* we belong to.

> At times we don't even realize where we are sowing the seed of the Gospel.

It is not impossible if we live each moment with the knowledge that He is closer to us than any family member, neighbor, or acquaintance, for the Holy Spirit of the Living God, whom we say we serve, resides within our hearts.

How are you scattering the seed of
the Gospel through your testimony
and praying that God will nourish it
with the Water of Life?

Set a watchtower in the midst of the vineyard. The
prophet Isaiah described the Lord's vineyard, declaring,
"He dug it up and cleared out its stones, and planted
it with the choicest vine. He built a tower in its midst.
. . . He expected it to bring forth good grapes, but it
brought forth wild grapes" (Isaiah 5:2).

Do we disappoint ourselves, and especially the
Lord, when the seed we sow produces bad instead of
good? The prophet spoke of setting a watchman in the
tower to report what was happening in the vineyard.
"My Lord, I stand continually on the watchtower in
the daytime; I have sat at my post every night" (Isaiah
21:8). For believers today, the vineyard is the world, and
it is rotting. God put His church in the midst of it and
commanded that His Word of the Gospel be sown. He

put His people in the midst of the vineyard to nourish the Gospel seed with the fountain of truth. How faithful are we to this task as we encounter those whose spirits are dried up by Satan's lies?

The apostle Paul encouraged God's people to defend the faith—God's Word. Are we observing from the watchtower with discernment? Are we a beacon of light from that watchtower in the midst of enemy territory? Do we stand for His holy way of life? Are we upholding the most basic principles of moral truth: the sanctity of marriage, protection of the unborn, righteousness in government, and the sacredness of His church? As we seek to do the will of God, let's pray to live in a way that pleases Him, remembering that our overseer is **Jesus, the Watchtower.**

At the beginning of the watches; pour out your heart like water before the face of the Lord. Lift your hands toward Him for the life of [the young].

Lamentations 2:19

JESUS
THE THORN-BEARER

And some seed fell among thorns; and the thorns grew up and choked it, and it yielded no crop.

Mark 4:7

If you've ever stepped into a briar patch, you understand what thorns do to human flesh. When you're fortunate enough to get untangled, the pinheads of the thorns seem to run with you. The only time in Scripture that a thorn was used for good comes from the apostle Paul: "Lest I should be exalted . . . a thorn in the flesh was given to me, a messenger of Satan to buffet me. . . . [The Lord] said to me, 'My grace is sufficient for you.' . . . Therefore most gladly, I will rather boast in my infirmities, that the power of Christ may rest upon me" (2 Corinthians 12:7–9).

We know that Paul did not have a literal thorn piercing his skin, but whatever his infirmity, it stung as though it was a thorn ripping the flesh. Paul identifies the "thorn" as a "messenger of Satan." No wonder the Bible speaks of thorns and snares, a wilderness of thorns, a fire of thorns, a hedge of thorns, and sadly—a crown of thorns. All of these were Satan's messengers. Jeremiah prophesied the words of the Lord: "Break up your fallow ground, and do not sow among thorns" (Jeremiah 4:3). The prophet challenged the hardened hearts of God's people to break up the thorn-sown ground and make it useful for sowing good seed.

We *reflect* on the darkness at Calvary when the Lord Jesus hung on the cross with a twisted "crown of thorns . . . on His head. . . . And they bowed the knee before Him and mocked Him, saying, "Hail, King of the Jews!" (Matthew 27:29). Jesus bore the thorns of our sin. But we also *rejoice* for the harvest is coming. There is healing from the piercing of the thorns. "Behold . . . on the cloud sat One like the Son of Man, having on His head a golden crown, and in His hand a sharp sickle. And another angel . . . crying with a loud voice to Him . . . 'Thrust in Your sickle and reap . . . for the harvest of the earth is ripe'" (Revelation 14:14–15).

> Break up the thorn-sown ground and make it useful for sowing good seed.

You see, there is hope. "At the name of Jesus every knee should bow . . . and every tongue should confess that Jesus Christ is Lord" (Philippians 2:10–11).

When the seed of the Gospel falls upon thorn-filled hearts, the truth is pricked against the thorn-seeded lies of Satan and a battle is waged for the soul. Satan will do all within his power to keep the seed from taking root, often victorious in winning a soul for his realm of everlasting darkness. Christians, through the power of Christ, must warn others of the briar patches that entrap the lost.

The Lord said to Ezekiel, "And you, son of man, do not be afraid of them nor be afraid of their words, though briars and thorns are with you. . . . You shall speak My words to them, whether they hear or whether they refuse" (Ezekiel 2:6–7).

> What will you do to spread the seed of the Gospel in the thorn-filled ground where others are walking?

Thorns are inevitable. They should not take us by surprise. We should be aware of them, because we are surrounded by deceit, lies, and corruption; these are the thorn bushes and prickly briars that entangle hearts and minds. They rip open flesh and draw blood. We see it splashed across the news by the hour. Racial bias inflames bigotry. Immorality engulfs even the young. Justification for breaking God's laws incites violence.

These are the thorny briars that choke the flow of joyful living.

Florists often de-thorn roses before plunging them into a water-filled vase creating a lush bouquet. Likewise, briars are snares that trap the water. So it is with the farmer who diligently works to de-thorn his field so that the briars will not choke out the life in the seed, allowing rain to seep into the soil. This is what happens when a sinner is transformed by Christ's salvation—the Vinedresser cuts away the thorns and dethrones Satan, bringing newness of life as we bow to the Master's way. Let the faith that heals trample out the thorns that wound. The One who heals our thorn pricks and bears our burdens, is **Jesus, the Thorn-bearer.**

Thorns and snares are in the way of the perverse; he who guards his soul will be far from them. . . . For every tree is known by its own fruit. For men do not gather figs from thorns, nor do they gather grapes from a bramble bush.

Proverbs 22:5; Luke 6:44

JESUS
THE SOUL SEEKER

But other seed fell on good ground and yielded a crop that sprang up, increased and produced: some thirtyfold, some sixty, and some a hundred.

Mark 4:8

The number of souls reached for the kingdom of God is incalculable. As the parable of the talents proclaims, the master does not hold his stewards responsible for the results, but He does reward them for their faithfulness (Matthew 25:23). We sow, we plant, and we water the seed of the Gospel with our prayers for the lost and our songs of praise for the saved.

All glory for the winning of souls belongs to the Savior of our souls, the Lord Jesus Christ; for even the seed—the Word of God—is given to the sower to spread around the world, scatter along the pathway, and plant deep into the hearts of mankind. The book of Isaiah says, "For as the rain comes down, and the snow from heaven . . . [to] water the earth, and make it bring forth and bud, that it may give seed to the sower . . . so shall My word be that goes

> All glory for the winning of souls belongs to the Savior of our souls.

forth from My mouth; it shall not return to Me void, but it shall accomplish what I please, and it shall prosper in the thing for which I sent it" (Isaiah 55:10–11).

Jesus set the example of what a sower of the seed is

to be. He sowed seed with each step He took. He said, "I am the light of the world. He who follows Me shall not walk in darkness, but have the light of life" (John 8:12). The footsteps of Jesus are sure, and because this is true, we can walk by faith with assurance that He is with us. "As you therefore have received Christ Jesus the Lord, so walk in Him, rooted and built up in Him and established in the faith" (Colossians 2:6–7). With great joy we can follow His example in sowing seeds of faith that lead others to the One who has sown His love into the fields where *truth* is planted.

The Bible says, "Those who sow in tears shall reap in joy. He who continually goes forth weeping, bearing seed for sowing, shall doubtless come again with rejoicing, bringing his sheaves with him" (Psalm 126:5–6).

Will you put Jesus Christ ahead of each step you take as you sow the seed of His Gospel through His fields of harvest?

The Gospel seed is packed with all that is needed for life—everlasting life! The seed is the very truth that flows from the mouth of God. While it is true that the heart of man is wicked and evil (Jeremiah 17:9), causing hearts to harden to the things of the Lord, the Bible also tells us that because of God's great love, He has planted knowledge of His very existence in the soil of human hearts. "What may be known of God is manifest in them, for God has shown it to them. For since the creation of the world His invisible attributes are clearly seen . . . so that [mankind is] without excuse, because, although they knew God, they did not glorify Him as God . . . but became futile in their thoughts, and their foolish hearts were darkened . . . [and] exchanged the truth of God for the lie" (Romans 1:19–21, 25).

The results rest with each individual as to whether the seed takes root, so do not become weary when you plant the seed. You may never know the end result in another's life until every redeemed soul stands before the God of heaven. We will cast our eyes not only on the harvest, but on the Lord of the harvest. And if you ever find yourself wondering just where the Gospel seed should be planted, remember the words of Jesus: "That repentance and remission of sins should be preached in [Jesus'] name to all nations" (Luke 24:47). As Jesus explained the Great Commission to His disciples, He "opened their understanding, that they might comprehend the Scriptures" (Luke 24:45). This is the work of **Jesus, the Soul Seeker.**

The fruit of the righteous is a tree of life, and he who wins souls is wise.

Proverbs 11:30

JESUS
THE PREACHER

And [Jesus] said to them, "He who has ears to hear, let him hear!"

Mark 4:9

When the Lord Jesus Christ taught in the synagogue, He read the Scriptures aloud, quoting from Isaiah: "'The Spirit of the LORD is upon Me, because He has anointed Me to preach the gospel to the poor; He has sent Me to heal the brokenhearted, to proclaim liberty to the captives and recovery of sight to the blind, to set at liberty those who are oppressed. . . . Today this Scripture is fulfilled in your hearing.' So all bore witness to Him, and marveled at the gracious words which proceeded out of His mouth" (Luke 4:18, 21–22).

Jesus was sowing the seed of the Gospel in the *most likely* location—a place of worship. He planted in the hearts of the hearers His reason for coming to earth in the form of man—so they could hear the Word of God.

He sowed the Gospel seed in many ways: with rich mercy in the hearts of the poor; with healing into broken hearts; with freedom to those in captivity; with light into the eyes of the blind; and with comfort to those who were oppressed. The hearers rejoiced at Jesus' words filled with hope and consolation—until He spoke of this same grace being extended to the Gentiles.

Suddenly those present did not want to hear the rest of the story. They were indignant. The Bible says they were "filled with wrath" (Luke 4:28).

This is what Jesus was saying in the parable of the sower. Many did not want to hear the truth, so they hardened the soil of their souls to His message. The Bible tells us that if we will open our hearts to God's Word, He will give understanding to the deaf and sight to the blind (Matthew 11:4–5).

> Is the soil of your soul prepared
> to receive what Christ
> desires to give?

Sowing the Gospel seed begins with obedience. If we really follow Jesus, if we really believe that the Spirit of God guides our footsteps, we will walk with Christ and sow seed at all times, because we are His workmen—His representatives on earth. Do we act like it? Do people see His light in our countenance? Do people hear our words that bear witness to His holiness? Do our actions demonstrate our obedience to His truth, even when we are wronged?

A woman once told a series of lies about another person. For some time the lies were believed by all who knew the young man, but he knew Christ and exhibited a strong faith, believing in the One who would make all things right. In time, the woman, who had been so convincing, was accused of a crime she did not commit. The young man appeared in court to testify on her behalf. She became convicted by his countenance and broke down, admitting that she had slandered him unmercifully. Another man, the boy's father, moved by the story, stood and also admitted that he had wrongfully accused the woman of the crime to avenge his son.

> Many did not want to hear the truth, so they hardened the soil of their souls to His message.

The Gospel seed of forgiveness had been sown by the very one who had been wronged. Restoration followed, and a strong witness for Christ reigned in the hearts of the people.

The Bible has a lot to say about liars. Scripture also strongly commends those who speak the truth: "A truthful witness saves lives, but one who breathes out lies is deceitful" (Proverbs 14:25 ESV). The Bible tells us not to take revenge, but to trust in God (Romans 12:19). "Behold, all those who were incensed against you shall be ashamed and disgraced. Fear not, I will help you" (Isaiah 41:11, 13). When we follow Christ's example, He will use what man intended for harm to bring glory to His Name.

This is the message of grace offered by **Jesus, the Preacher.**

> *He who goes out weeping, bearing the seed for sowing, shall come home with shouts of joy.*
>
> *Psalm 126:6 ESV*

JESUS
THE DISCERNER OF HEARTS

But when [Jesus] was alone, those around Him with the twelve asked Him about the parable.

Mark 4:10

J esus knew the hardened hearts of those who turned away. Many came hoping to see miracles. They wanted to be *wowed* by watching a lame man walk; they wanted to watch the thrill of a blind man opening his eyes to faces he had never seen. There is nothing wrong with wanting to see the miracle-working Teacher in action, but the crowd around Jesus wanted only the breathtaking amazement of witnessing Jesus at work. They were not interested in learning the lessons He was sowing along the sun-drenched paths He trod. The Bible says, "The natural man does not receive the things of the Spirit of God, for they are foolishness to him; nor can he know them, because they are spiritually discerned" (1 Corinthians 2:14). "They will turn their ears away from the truth" (2 Timothy 4:4).

When Jesus was alone with those who sincerely desired the truth, He patiently explained the meaning of the parable.

But when Jesus was alone with those who sincerely desired the truth, He patiently explained the meaning of the parable. The Lord knows the intention of our hearts, and it's important that we seek understanding of His Word. The parables teach about the one sowing the Word of God, the one hearing God's Word, and the One who is the Word of God: "In the beginning was the Word, and the Word was with God, and the Word was God" (John 1:1).

Most parents are overjoyed when a child comes asking for help with his homework. Parents want their children to learn; they cannot successfully comprehend many things without instruction, nor can adults understand all things. The Lord must have been pleased when those close to Him asked for further explanation. The psalmist said, "Teach me Your way, O Lord; I will walk in Your truth" (Psalm 86:11).

The Lord promised that He would send the Spirit to teach us (John 14:26).

Are you listening to what the Sower of the seed is teaching?

Playing tricks with God won't work. Ananias and Sapphira conspired to deceive the early church, as revealed in the book of Acts, by giving money from a piece of property they sold. They withheld a portion for themselves while claiming to have given it all. Peter perceived their evil deed and said: "Why has Satan filled your heart to lie to the Holy Spirit and to keep back part of the price of the land for yourself? Why have you conceived this thing in your heart? You have not lied to men but to God" (Acts 5:3–4). They seemed oblivious that God was watching, for they were seeking honor and approval from their peers. They were an integral part of the church, but by their actions they revealed their indifference that God knew the intentions of their hearts. They were struck down by the Lord Himself. They sought glory out of deception. Instead, their deception and greed brought death.

The privilege of belonging to Christ's church on earth is no small thing—it should be everything for believers, because conducting God's business must be done in truth. There is no room in the church for worldly ways. The Bible says, "Do not be conformed to this world, but be transformed by the renewal of your mind, that by testing you may discern what is the will of God, what is good and acceptable and perfect" (Romans 12:2 ESV). How do we demonstrate our desire to have obedient hearts for the Lord? Scripture instructs us to pray for the power of discernment, which comes by training and "constant practice to distinguish good from evil" (Hebrews 5:14 ESV). Let's not fail **Jesus, the Discerner of Hearts.**

For the word of God is living and powerful . . . and is a discerner of the thoughts and intents of the heart.

Hebrews 4:12

JESUS
THE SOWER OF UNDERSTANDING

And [Jesus] said to them, "To you it has been given to know the mystery of the kingdom of God; but to those who are outside, all things come in parables."

Mark 4:11

People tend to hear only what they want to hear. Jesus recognized this dimension of human nature, realizing that few desired to know the deeper meaning of what He said. It wasn't the parables, but the nuggets of truth in them that they turned their ears from. Jesus said, "Unless a grain of wheat falls into the ground and dies, it remains alone; but if it dies, it produces much grain" (John 12:24). To farmers this principle was clear, but to those who had never turned a spade of soil, the lesson could be missed. Paul picked up on this when he said, "What you sow is not made alive unless it dies" (1 Corinthians 15:36), teaching the principle that when seed is planted in the ground, it dies and regenerates, bringing new life.

Jesus said, "A little while longer the light is with you. . . . I still have many things to say to you, but you cannot bear them now . . . a little while, and you will not see Me; and again a little while, and you will see Me, because I go to the Father" (John 12:35; 16:12, 16). The disciples did not understand until He said, "I say to you that you will weep and lament, but the world will rejoice; and you will be sorrowful, but your sorrow will be turned into joy. . . . The time is coming when I will no longer speak to you in figurative language, but I will tell you plainly about the Father. . . . I came forth from the Father and have come into the world. Again, I leave the world and go to the Father" (John 16:20, 25, 28).

Jesus identified Himself as the Light of the World, but He predicted that the world would rejoice at His death, even though the grave would hold Him only to His appointed time—three days. He told the disciples that they would abandon Him out of fear—leaving Him alone. Then He foretold of His coming resurrection to life anew. This truth would give final and eternal explanation to the principle of the grain of wheat that dies in order to produce much grain (fruit). For in Jesus' death and resurrection, the truth He had implanted in others brought forth seed that was scattered abroad, producing laborers for the fields and fruit for the kingdom.

> In Jesus' death and resurrection, the truth He had implanted in others brought forth seed that was scattered abroad.

Likewise, "The body is *sown* in corruption, it is raised in incorruption. It is *sown* in dishonor, it is raised in glory. It is *sown* in weakness, it is raised in power. It is *sown* a natural body, it is raised in a spiritual body" (1 Corinthians 15:42–44).

Are you allowing the seed of the Gospel
to bring new life so that others
may live as fruit of your labor?

God's Word speaks to every heart that will listen. What about you? Do you desire to understand God's message? Do you want more than anything to comprehend the power that God's Spirit will demonstrate through you? If so, are you willing to obey? You see, the Bible calls us to follow Christ, who died and rose to life anew so that we can have life everlasting. Just as the seed dies when planted in the soil and then springs up again, we are called as the seed of Jesus Christ to die to ourselves so that we can live for Him. Satan does not want this to happen. He whispers in our ears for us to carry on as though Christ makes no marked difference in our walk, our talk, and our thoughts. His intention is to at least make us ineffective Christians so that our testimony cannot reach another soul with the Gospel. This seed must not remain dormant waiting for heaven; it is designed to blossom here and now! God promises to water the seed, restoring it for use. When we are obedient in setting aside our own desires and purposes, the Lord finds us faithful spades in His hand, for **Jesus is the Sower of Understanding.**

> *The Lord searches all hearts and understands all the intent of the thoughts.*
>
> *1 Chronicles 28:9*

JESUS
THE REJECTED ONE

. . . So that "seeing they may see and not perceive, and hearing they may hear and not understand; lest they should turn, and their sins be forgiven them."

Mark 4:12

Jesus offers all people the gift of His forgiving love. What makes mankind reject God's salvation? Many answers could be offered, but they would *all* boil down to this: Men love darkness rather than light because their deeds are evil (John 3:19).

The Bible says, "For *all* have sinned and fall short of the glory of God" (Romans 3:23). In order for people to accept God, they must first admit that they are sinners condemned before the righteous Judge. It is hard for many to reconcile that the righteous Judge is also the God of love. Human nature tends to gravitate toward excuses—*If God loves me, He will make me good. . . . If He loves me, He certainly won't condemn me.*

This is what Jesus was saying to His listeners. Those who rejected His truth were more than satisfied to take the food He offered when He fed the five thousand, but they did not want to feed on His Word. They wanted to be recipients of His miracle-working power, but they did not want to suffer

> Human nature tends to gravitate toward excuses.

for His name's sake. They wanted to enjoy the riches of eternal life, but they did not want to lay down their sinful lives in exchange for sacrificial and holy lives.

Jesus used parables to draw the true believers out of the crowd. Those who didn't care to understand simply turned away. Those who sought for truth begged, "Tell us more!" Some saw the miracles but chose to ignore their purpose. They saw, but did not perceive. They heard, but did not understand. If they would only choose to identify with Him and turn from their sins, they would be forgiven, but their willing sinfulness bound them to the world's empty lies. These represent the soil of unrepentant hearts in which the seed of the Gospel cannot take root.

Are you praying for Jesus
to cultivate the soil of unrepentant
hearts so that the seed of the Gospel
will take root and flourish?

No one likes to be rejected—no one! For believers, though, it is something that we should train for, because the Bible promises that just as our Savior was rejected by the world, so will those who follow Him be rejected. Satan wants us to live in a state of rejection and terror. Around the world, believers in Christ are being persecuted through imprisonment and beheadings. We have seen believers in the Western world shot to death because they dared to speak the name of Jesus Christ. And this is happening in what we call "a civilized world."

But my friend, do not be deceived. Satan is not sitting quietly on the sidelines of civilization. He tells us that we deserve better. He tells us that God should not require us to bear hostility from the world. Remember, Satan had the audacity to tell Jesus that He deserved more than what His Father in heaven offered. Satan is out in full measure prowling the earth to find victims to devour. Let's be careful not to overlook his devious ways. He exploits himself through gang violence and racial division. He doesn't just manifest himself in the chaos of political debates or in the confusion caused by gender transformation, cleverly changing the meaning of marriage, or excusing murder through abortion. His demonstrations of wickedness are not always clothed in darkness.

The Bible warns us that Satan's greatest deception

is posing as an angel of light. He is the bright and colorful neon light that beckons men and women into dens of sin. His spirit bubbles in the glass that causes anger to flare and tongues to curse. He walks the halls of government, prodding elected officials to exchange God's law for anarchy. And more concerning is when he slips unaware into our churches, watering down God's Gospel and persuading people to diminish biblical doctrine—God's truth that has been given to us for protection and guidance. This enemy—the devil and his demon band—must be revealed and rejected. Jesus said, "If they persecuted Me, they will also persecute you" (John 15:20). Let's not forget that as we sow the seed of God's Word, many will reject Christ and choose to go Satan's way. Nevertheless, let's walk with Christ no matter what, for **Jesus, the Rejected One** has been revealed as the Victor and will reign as King.

The Lord Jesus Christ [gave] Himself for our sins so that He might deliver us from this present evil age.

Galatians 1:3–4 ESV

JESUS
THE STORYTELLER

And [Jesus] said to them, "Do you not understand this parable? How then will you understand all the parables?"

Mark 4:13

Jesus taught infallible truth in parable form. His parables were not concocted stories; they were lessons meticulously wrapped in the law of God and tied together with heavenly hope. "Give ear, O my people, to my law; incline your ears to the words of my mouth. I will open my mouth in a parable; I will utter dark sayings of old . . . make them known . . . that the generation to come might know them . . . that they may set their hope in God, and not forget the works of God" (Psalm 78:1–2, 5–7). This was written centuries before the Lord Jesus walked upon the earth in human form, and here we see a prophecy fulfilled in the parable of the sower and "all the parables."

Among the evidence that the Bible is infallible is the fact that the inspired writers did not cover up the truth of even their own sin, referred to as "dark sayings of old." At one time or another, we all tell on ourselves. This is clearly revealed in the pages of Scripture. Many think of a storyteller as one who exaggerates the facts. Jesus—the sinless One—holds His listeners spellbound by *His story* . . . for He knows human nature like no other, and biblical *history* gives account to the sinless One, redeeming the sinful . . . one by one.

Someone defined a parable as "an earthly story with a heavenly meaning." Parables have greater impact when seen in the light of man's iniquity and God's infallibility. We see this in the parable of the lost son, which is a clear picture of the Lord welcoming a repentant child *home*.

This young man sowed wild seed—he lost his joy of living—but then he returned to his father.

Do you know some who are sowing
the wrong seed in the wrong field?
Are you praying for them
to return home to the Sower?

The crowd listened intently to Jesus' story. They likely gasped within as He described the prodigal son, perhaps the most famed example of rebellion and redemption. It was despicable in that society for a son to dishonor his father, bringing shame to the family name. The Bible tells us that "Those who plow iniquity and sow trouble reap the same" (Job 4:8). The young man who demanded his inheritance while his father still lived, took the money and lived it up, sowing for himself carelessness, carousing godlessly, boasting of wealth he had not earned, and buying friends—at least as long as the money held out. Then he hit the rocks. His friends deserted him and he had to resort to cleaning up after the pigs to earn meager wages to eat. He was reaping the result of sowing bad seed. "Whoever sows injustice will reap calamity" (Proverbs 22:8 ESV).

While in the pigpen of the world, he "came to himself" and returned to his father's house of plenty, where he found forgiveness and acceptance. The son had humbled himself and offered to be only a servant on his father's estate. Instead, the father received him back as his beloved son and celebrated his return. This is a picture of the sinner and the forgiving Father. When the father saw his boy walking toward home, we can imagine the father must have realized that the seed he had sown through prayer for his son was sprouting with life. Parables, indeed, have greater impact when told by **Jesus, the Storyteller.**

> Someone defined a parable as "an earthly story with a heavenly meaning."

Light is sown for the righteous, and gladness for the upright in heart.

Psalm 97:11

JESUS
IDENTIFIES
THE SEED

The sower sows the word.

Mark 4:14

Jesus describes the seed as "the Word of God" (Luke 8:11). As Jesus trekked throughout the land and saw great numbers following Him, He opened His mouth with parables—and plowed the soil of human hearts, planting seed—the very words of God.

If you were to circle common phrases in many of Jesus' parables you would make this discovery: There are *kingdom* threads woven through the parables. They aren't clever thoughts; they are clear truths. The Lord was not entertaining the throngs. He was sowing *kingdom* seed.

"The kingdom of heaven *is like a man* who sowed good seed . . ." (Matthew 13:24); "The kingdom of heaven *is like a mustard seed*, which a man took and sowed in his field . . ." (Matthew 13:31); "The kingdom of heaven *is like* leaven, which *a woman* took and hid . . ." (Matthew 13:33); "The kingdom of heaven *is like treasure* hidden in a field . . ." (Matthew 13:44); "The kingdom of heaven *is like a merchant* seeking beautiful pearls . . . " (Matthew 13:45); "The kingdom of heaven *is like a dragnet* that was cast into the sea . . ." (Matthew 13:47); "The kingdom of heaven *is like a certain king* who wanted to settle accounts with his servants . . ." (Matthew 18:23); "The kingdom of heaven *is like a landowner* who went out early in the morning to hire laborers for his vineyard . . ." (Matthew 20:1); "The kingdom of heaven *is like* a *certain king* who arranged a marriage for his son, and sent out his servants to call those who were invited to the wedding . . ." (Matthew 22:2–3); "The kingdom of heaven *shall be likened to ten virgins* who . . . went out to meet the bridegroom . . ." (Matthew 25:1); "For the kingdom of heaven *is like a man* traveling to a far country, who called his own servants and delivered his goods to them . . ." (Matthew 25:14).

> These are not fairy tales. Jesus gives us glimpses of His kingdom.

These are not fairy tales. Jesus gives us glimpses of His kingdom. Jesus speaks of individuals: merchants, land owners, laborers, and kings. Jesus tells of far countries and vineyards. He tells of hidden treasures, settling accounts, and delivering goods. He tells of weddings . . . and the bridegroom. Simply put, He is sowing the seed of the Gospel of His kingdom in the hearts of the hearers.

<hr />

How has the Sower planted the seed
of the Gospel in your heart
through these parables?

<hr />

The kingdom of heaven is like a strong tower. It is filled
with all that is good, righteous, and holy because Jesus
abides there as the King of glory. The abundance of fruit
from the seed of His Gospel will fill heaven with truth,
because Christ does transform broken and shattered
lives. There will be no weeds from wicked seed in His
presence, for no sin will preside in His heavenly home.
Who would not want to enjoy such an eternity?

Believe it or not, people in their darkened state
actually claim they look forward to hell. Then there are
others who believe that God receives every person no
matter their unwillingness to repent and accept His gift
of salvation. They believe that as long as they do good
things they will get to heaven. Make no mistake; there is
an eternal penalty to pay for the rejection of Christ. The
tares sown by sin on earth will be gathered and thrown
into utter darkness, where they will burn throughout
eternity.

The Bible says, "You have sown much, and harvested little. You eat, but you never have enough; you drink, but you never have your fill. You clothe yourselves, but no one is warm. And he who earns wages does so to put them into a bag with holes" (Haggai 1:6 ESV). Make certain that the seed that you are watering, with your thoughts and deeds, is from *Jesus, who identifies the seed* as the Gospel truth.

These dreamers defile the flesh, reject authority, and speak evil of dignitaries . . . serving only themselves. They are clouds without water, carried about by the winds; late autumn trees without fruit, twice dead, pulled up the roots; raging waves of the sea, foaming up their own shame; wandering stars for whom is reserved the blackness of darkness forever. . . . But you, beloved, remember the words . . . keep yourselves in the love of God, looking for the mercy of our Lord Jesus Christ unto eternal life.

Jude 8, 12–13, 17, 21

JESUS
IDENTIFIES
THE THIEF

And these are the ones by the wayside where the word is sown. When they hear, Satan comes immediately and takes away the word that was sown in their hearts.

Mark 4:15

Luke records the same account this way: "Those by the wayside are the ones who hear; then the devil comes and takes away the word out of their hearts, lest they should believe and be saved" (8:12). This is *stolen seed.*

Satan will do everything in his power to turn a soul away from the Lord "according to the working of Satan, with all power, signs, and lying wonders, and with all unrighteous deception among those who perish, because they did not receive the love of the truth, that they might be saved" (2 Thessalonians 2:9–10).

This is the business that Satan is in, and he's good at it. But take careful note that while Satan is powerful, he is not *all-powerful*, for that is a realm that belongs only to God (Job 2:6). The Bible says that God will destroy Satan, who has the power of death, releasing those subject to bondage (Hebrews 2:14).

> Satan will do everything in his power to turn a soul away from the Lord.

Jesus sent the apostle Paul to the people of the world to sow "the love of the truth" because they were in bondage to Satan's lies. The Lord was blessing His Word through Paul's ministry "to turn them from darkness to light, and from the power of Satan to God, that they may receive forgiveness of sins . . . by faith in Me" (Acts 26:18).

But as convincing as Paul was, some mocked him and turned away (Acts 17:32). This illustrates the seed of the Word of God that is stolen by Satan.

Are you praying for those who are in Satan's clutches, that the seed will penetrate and take root in their hearts?

Don't let discouragement get you off track. Many believers who spread the Gospel seed allow Satan to have victory even in their lives. How? When we evangelize—sow God's truth into the lives of others—we put the emphasis on our own effort instead of the power of the Living God. The Word may take root in the hearts of unbelievers until the world's ways tug and pull, convincing them that they will have to give up too much to follow the way of Christ. What are we to do? Pray. Ask God to protect the seed of the Gospel planted in their hearts. Water the seed of truth with prayer to drive the thieves away from hearts that struggle between good and evil.

The apostle Paul reminded the early church that he had not ceased to warn them night and day of thieves who come in and steal away God's truth from those that might believe. (Acts 20: 31) Pray that the Gospel seed will not only take root, but flourish in the lives of those who hear. As we follow Him we must do as **Jesus did: Identify the thief** and encourage the sinner to turn toward the truth.

Whoever is a partner with a thief hates his own life; he swears to tell the truth, but reveals nothing. . . . The thief does not come except to steal, and to kill, and to destroy. I have come that they may have life, and that they may have it more abundantly.

Proverbs 29:24; John 10:10

JESUS
PROCLAIMS

These likewise are the ones sown on stony ground who, when they hear the word, immediately receive it with gladness.

Mark 4:16

Imagine Paul standing before King Agrippa, the son of King Herod who had the apostle James beheaded. Paul had been arrested for preaching Christ and was brought before Agrippa to defend himself. The king said, "You are permitted to speak" (Acts 26:1). What an opportunity! How did Paul respond? He sowed the seed of the Gospel in the heart of the king. He lived out Psalm 119:46: "I will speak of Your testimonies also before kings." Paul boldly asked, "King Agrippa, do you believe the prophets?" (Acts 26:27).

Paul knew that if Agrippa said yes, the king would give indication that he believed in the One the prophets predicted would come—the One whom Paul proclaimed. Then Agrippa said to Paul, "You almost persuade me to become a Christian" (Acts 26:28).

Agrippa was captivated by the Word of God. He even thought Paul was innocent of the charges against him. The seed of truth had fallen into the soil of the king's heart, but he didn't take hold of it—the seed did not take root. He "did not believe in God, and did not trust in His salvation" (Psalm 78:22). This is the picture of *wasted seed*. "So are the paths of all who forget God. . . .

his roots wrap around the rock heap, and look for a place in the stones" (Job 8:13, 17).

Whether we speak before royalty or relatives, friends or foes, the Bible says, "Come and hear, all you who fear God, and I will declare what He has done for my soul" (Psalm 66:16). This testimony of the power of God in our lives is a faith-packed seed that has the potential of taking root in another's heart.

Whether it does or doesn't, exercise the right to speak, as Paul did.

Will you pray, as Paul did in
Acts 26:29, that all who hear
the truth might become Christians?

Our culture today ridicules the Christian faith and debates about what it means to be a Christian. If you were arrested for being a Christian, would there be enough evidence to convict you? Many people say they are Christians, but there is no fruit to demonstrate that their lives have been changed by Christ. They know the language of the church and many boast of their works, but they do not know Him as Lord and Master. This is catastrophic. Satan, the thief, is pleased when he has tricked others into thinking that just because they claim to be Christians they are saved. They are recipients of the seed of truth, but their lives do not produce its sweet fruit. Because they claim to know Jesus, they think they have the card that will keep them out of hell.

> The power of God in our lives is a faith-packed seed that has the potential of taking root in another's heart.

The Bible says, "For the one who sows to his own flesh will from the flesh reap corruption, but the one who sows to the Spirit will from the Spirit reap eternal life" (Galatians 6:8 ESV). How do we know we belong to Christ? The apostle John tells us: "Whoever does not practice righteousness is not of God" (1 John 3:10); "Whoever confesses that Jesus is the Son of God, God abides in him, and he in God" (1 John 4:15).

God empowers those who belong to Him to be overcomers through His abiding Spirit. Those who seek to please themselves are of the world. They understand worldliness. But those who know God hear the truth and abide in it (1 John 4:6). Let's pray for those who struggle with having one foot in the world and another in the field of indecision. Pray that they will settle their place in eternity with **Jesus who proclaims . . .**

The kingdom of God is at hand. Repent, and believe in the gospel.

Mark 1:15

JESUS
KNOWS

. . . They have no root in themselves, and so endure only for a time. Afterward, when tribulation or persecution arises for the word's sake, immediately they stumble.

Mark 4:17

The word "immediately" is used four times in the parable of the sower. *Immediately*, without thought or reflection, they receive the Word of God, but the first time trials come because of their association with God's Word, they falter. Their faith in God is on shallow ground, and they stumble over rocks of disbelief. They presented themselves on the outside as Christians, but there was no connection to the power of God's Word to help them overcome. Instead of relying on what they claimed to believe, they turned away—the seed did not take root. Just as the Old Testament records Israel's rejection of good, the Bible says, "The enemy will pursue him. . . . They sow the wind, and reap the whirlwind" (Hosea 8:3, 7).

> Their faith in God is on shallow ground, and they stumble over rocks of disbelief.

As Jesus sowed His Word into the hearts of His listeners, He knew where the seed was taking root and where seed was blowing in the wind. "He who eats this bread [the Word of God] will live forever. . . . Does this offend you?" Jesus asked (John 6:58, 61). "The words that I speak to you are spirit and they are life. But there are some of you who do not believe" (John 6:63–64). Some resented that He knew the intent of their hearts and their lack of belief—and from that time, many of His followers "walked with Him no more" (John 6:66).

Others who claim salvation in Christ walk with the Lord while life is good. But when life doesn't meet their expectations—whether it's due to bad health, a lost job, or a wayward child—they abandon the faith and "[walk] with Him no more." This is what Jesus was saying in the parable: "When tribulation or persecution arises because of the word, *immediately* he stumbles" (Matthew 13:21). The seed had landed on stony ground.

Will you pray and ask the Lord
to direct the Gospel seed you
are casting along your paths?

Ten men begged to be healed. Jesus was passing by as they called out to Him. He stopped. He listened to their plea. And He told them what to do. *Immediately*, they were cleansed of leprosy. And *immediately* one man returned to thank the Lord. Jesus said, "Were there not ten cleansed? But where are the nine? (Luke 17:17). Like vultures, the pack of nine took what satisfied their desire and *immediately* returned to their former life, never giving thanks to the One who had given them new life. Only one man, urgently and without delay, returned to Jesus and worshiped at His feet, giving glory to God.

The Bible says, "Lay aside all filthiness and overflow of wickedness, and receive with meekness the implanted word, which is able to save your souls. But be doers of the word, and not hearers only, deceiving yourselves. For if anyone is a hearer of the word and not a doer, he is like a man observing his natural face in a mirror, for he observes himself, goes away, and *immediately* forgets what kind of man he was. But he who looks . . . and is not a forgetful hearer but a doer of the word, this one will be blessed" (James 1:21–25).

We remember the story of Paul's conversion. The Bible says, "Immediately . . . he arose and was baptized . . . immediately he preached [that] Christ . . . is the Son of God" (Acts 9:18, 20). Pray that those who receive the Word of God will thank Him and begin walking by faith in Christ that brings an immediate life change, for **Jesus knows** His own.

Jesus said, "I am the good shepherd; and I know My sheep, and am known by My own."

John 10:14

JESUS
OBSERVES
THE HEARERS

Now these are the ones sown among thorns;

they are the ones who hear the word. . . .

Mark 4:18

Jesus described seed that falls into the hearts of four types of people: the first, "the ones who hear" (Luke 8:12); the second, "when they hear" (Luke 8:13); the third, "when they have heard" (Luke 8:14); and the last, "having heard the word" (Luke 8:15). This is a wonderful picture of the Word of God being "heard." The not-so-wonderful picture is what three types of people do with what they have heard. The first group hears the truth but doesn't embrace it, welcoming in the thief. The second group hears the truth and welcomes it, but when the thrill wears off, they wander away. The third group hears but welcomes worldly distractions that crowd their minds and feed their desires. The fourth group hears the Word and feeds on it, causing the good seed to bear good fruit.

This third group has something in common with the children of Israel. They were thriving, sowing seeds of pleasure for themselves and bearing no fruit. The Bible says, "They have sown wheat but reaped thorns . . . be ashamed of your harvest" (Jeremiah 12:13). "Tremble, you [who] are at ease . . . beat your breasts for the pleasant fields . . . for the soil of my people growing up in thorns and briars" (Isaiah 32:11–13 ESV)

Many churchgoers today are in this category. They have heard the Word of God, yet they mix the Word with error, feeding on worldly pleasures that choke the truth and drain the life out of the seed. This group often goes unnoticed by God's people, who assume they are obedient followers of Christ.

The truth is that Satan plants bad seed inside the church, introducing distractions that trample and bruise the good seed of God's Word. Satan cannot pluck the root of good seed from God's fields of harvest, but he can and does sow tares (pretenders) in our churches, many times rendering God's people ineffective because they, too, become distracted by things other than the Word of the living God. They "have run greedily in [error] . . . while they feast with you without fear, serving only themselves. They are . . . late autumn trees without fruit, twice dead, pulled up by the roots; raging waves of the sea, foaming up their own shame" (Jude 11–13).

> They have heard the Word of God, yet they mix the Word with error.

Will you pray for wisdom to distinguish
Satan's bad seed and rotten fruit from
the fruit of the Spirit that blossoms
from the good seed of God's Word?

Don't drink the Kool-Aid. Truth versus lies. Right versus wrong. Good versus evil. Disciples versus deceivers. We see a jolting comparison between how God's people should live and those who live in the devil's trap and don't know it. That dirty old bird—Satan—poses as an angel of light, but he doesn't tread lightly. He tramples and destroys. The Bible tells us he is the prince of darkness and his kingdom is the pagan world. The Scripture also identifies Jesus Christ as the coming Prince of Peace. But until He comes again, believers are entrenched in a hostile world. Take confidence. Jesus is greater than he who is in the world (1 John 4:4).

Jesus empowers His followers to do right; Satan deceives his followers and persuades them to do wrong but calls it right. Truth mixed with error is nothing but error—a tangled briar. Beware! When error is present, mankind fails to distinguish one from the other. Truth mixed with lies is poison. But that is only half of the story. Poison kills the body, but the devil's mixed drink is a potion that is deceptive and deadly to the eternal soul.

Many recall Jim Jones, a charismatic man who posed as an evangelist and convinced his followers to drink themselves to death as they ingested cyanide-laced Kool-Aid. It was in the aftermath of the Jonestown Massacre that the metaphor was coined: "Don't drink the Kool-Aid." The Bible tells us to beware of those "having a form of godliness but denying its power . . . from such people turn away" (2 Timothy 3:5).

Deceivers will proclaim that there is no room in Christianity for judgment. Don't be duped. Without right judgment we cannot distinguish error. We are called to defend the faith from error, and we are to live a life that does not mix truth and error, for the Bible says, "What communion has light and darkness?" (2 Corinthians 6:14).

The eyes of God are fixed upon the fields of the world and His ears are attentive as **Jesus observes the hearers.**

> *[Those who] are of the world . . . speak as of the world, and the world hears them. We are of God. He who knows God hears us; he who is not of God does not hear us. By this we know the spirit of truth and the spirit of error.*
>
> *1 John 4:5–6*

JESUS
THE WAY

. . . And the cares of this world, the deceitfulness of riches, and the desires for other things entering in choke the word, and it becomes unfruitful.

Mark 4:19

This verse mirrors the reality of the rich young ruler who asked Jesus, "Good Teacher, what shall I do to inherit eternal life?" (Mark 10:17). This young man obviously had heard God's Word and thought he was a prime candidate for the gift Jesus offered—eternal life. He thought he was good enough to enter into God's promise of forgiveness, without repenting. This is *selfish seed*. But when Jesus looked at him *with love* and told him that he lacked one thing, "Go *your way*, sell whatever you have . . . take up the cross, and follow Me" (Mark 10:21), the young man's feet were planted firmly in the soil of his *own way*. He wasn't willing to exchange his way for God's way. Jesus said, "I am the way" (John 14:6). The deceitfulness of riches had choked the Word of God, which says, "Here is the man who did not make God his strength, but trusted in the abundance of his riches" (Psalm 52:7). It wasn't the young man's wealth that was wrong; it was his loyalty to his riches that was wrong. He couldn't serve two masters. "No one can serve two masters; for either he will hate the one and love the other, or else he will be loyal to the one and despise the other. You cannot serve God and mammon" (Matthew 6:24). He wasn't willing to lay aside *his way* for *the way*.

Life is richer when seeds of selflessness are sown. Doing good unto others, as the Bible commands, reaps a bountiful harvest. This is what the young man would have learned if he had chosen to follow Jesus instead of being enslaved by his riches. He would have learned that the seed Jesus was about to sow at Calvary would sprout in his heart. The path to Calvary was going to seed the fertile soil of searching souls and bring forth the fruit of eternal life. "Do not be deceived, God is not mocked; for whatever a man sows, that he will also reap. For he who sows to his flesh will of the flesh reap corruption, but he who sows to the Spirit will of the Spirit reap everlasting life" (Galatians 6:7–8).

Are you ready to sow the seed
of God's truth in others when they ask,
"What must I do to inherit everlasting life?"

Salvation is God's provision. Some people use God's gift for personal gain. They believe salvation will cancel out pain, suffering, and loss, receiving in return good health, joy, and wealth. Those who see life from a carnal and worldly point of view believe that salvation fulfills fleshly desires. Salvation, my friend, is deeper than flesh—much deeper. When Christ comes into a life, He changes it for His purpose—not ours. It is a change that illuminates the unseen—the soul. When we truly repent of our sin against holy God, He empowers us to live godly lives without becoming tangled in the briars of the world. He

> The path to Calvary was going to seed the fertile soil of searching souls and bring forth the fruit of eternal life.

gives us an eternal view. When we stand with God, we understand that "the whole world lies under the sway of the wicked one" (1 John 5:19).

Danger lurks, and sorrow rattles like a saber when people pretend to accept Christ but bail at the first sign of trouble. The Bible says, "Do not be surprised at the fiery trial when it comes upon you to test you . . . but rejoice insofar as you share Christ's sufferings, that you may also rejoice and be glad when his glory is revealed. If you are insulted for the name of Christ, you are blessed, because the Spirit of glory and of God rests upon you. If anyone suffers as a Christian, let him not be ashamed, but let him glorify God in that name" (1 Peter 4:12–14, 16).

It is often in trying times that we are given a chance to sow seed in unlikely places. Plant it with truth. Let's not clothe salvation in lies, but honestly testify that God's eternal redemption will see us through the storms of life with unspeakable joy. Let's not settle for just a happy life when we can attain holy living that pleases God. Man cannot serve two masters for, "a double-minded man [is] unstable in all his ways" (James 1:8). Jesus told His own to follow Him. It does not mean to only follow Him to heaven; it means to follow Him through rough waters, through doubt, and through disappointment. Then, when our time on earth ends, we will follow Him to the glory, wonder, and certainty of heaven's eternity, for **Jesus is the only Way.**

> *Jesus said, "I am the way, the truth, and the life. No one comes to the Father except through Me."*
>
> *John 14:6*

JESUS,
THE LIFE-GIVING VINE

But these are the ones sown on good ground, those who hear the word, accept it, and bear fruit: some thirtyfold, some sixty, and some a hundred.

Mark 4:20

We can picture Jesus at this moment, perhaps with a smile on His face, as He spoke of the seed yielding abundant fruit. He had delivered some soul-searching thoughts to those hearing this parable, and it must have pleased the Lord to speak of the good fruit that comes from the good seed—souls harvested from preaching the Gospel. *This is yielded seed*—hearts emptied of all distractions of the world and dedicated to the things of Christ. Hearts emptied of self-pleasure and spilling over with a desire to pursue the lost. Hearts drained of the cares of life and filled with continual praise to the Lord.

Perhaps when Jesus concluded this parable, He was picturing heaven filled with the fruits of the vine. After all, He had told His followers, "I am the vine, you are the branches. He who abides in Me, and I in him, bears much fruit" (John 15:5). He also told them, "I go to prepare a place for you" (John 14:2). No one can fathom the harvest of plenty to come.

In His Word the Lord has given us all that we need for this life. But Scripture tells us that "there are also many other things that Jesus did, which if they were written one by one . . . even the world itself could not contain the books that would be written" (John 21:25). This truth should compel us to be effective sowers and bountiful fruit-bearers.

Is your heart plowed, prepared,
and planted with the good seed
of God's Word?

He was the most notable Pharisee to seek after Jesus. In the cover of night, Nicodemus searched for Him, wanting to know if Jesus was telling the truth about who He was. And Nicodemus found Him! Jesus threaded the needle and began sowing truth, proving He was the promised Savior sent from heaven. He declared, "Nicodemus, you must be born again!" As the needle and thread went deeper into the heart of this seeker, Jesus nourished the seed with the richness and fullness of truth: "For God so loved the world that He gave His only begotten Son, that whoever believes in Him should not perish but have everlasting life" (John 3:16). Jesus continued, "For everyone practicing evil hates the light and does not come to the light, lest his deeds should be exposed. But he who does the truth comes to the light, that his deeds may be clearly seen, that they have been done in God" (John 3:20–21). How interesting that Nicodemus went in search of Jesus in the dark of night to find the Light of truth.

While Scripture does not tell us how the "undercover" meeting ended, the next time Nicodemus is mentioned in Scripture he was witnessing to his peers on behalf of Jesus (John 7). Later,

> This truth should compel us to be effective sowers and bountiful fruit-bearers.

we are told that he assisted Joseph of Arimathea in Christ's burial, giving us indication that the seed Jesus had planted within Nicodemus had taken root and blossomed. Jesus tells us to "go and do likewise." Sow the seed of the Gospel and pray for a bountiful harvest, for **Jesus is the Life-Giving Vine.**

> *If you seek Him, He will be found by you; but if you forsake Him, He will cast you off forever. . . . Jesus said, "I am the true vine. . . . He who abides in Me, and I in Him, bears much fruit; for without Me you can do nothing."*
>
> *1 Chronicles 28:9; John 15:1, 5*

REAPING
THE NINE FRUITS
OF THE SPIRIT

The Boundless Rot of Sin and the Bountiful Fruits of the Spirit

Nine pillars of history develop a successful society, so it is claimed. Some have written about the Nine noble virtues. More valuable than these are the Nine bountiful fruits of the Spirit that reap the abundant favor of God and burst with flavor from the seed of the Gospel. These are the virtues of the Lord Jesus Christ. **We are told to seek them, pray to possess them, and live to exemplify them.** Scripture shines a light on God's attributes.

In contrast, God's Word does not hide the evil deeds of the wicked. This boundless rot of sin is manifested from the original sin that took place in the beginning—the sin of disobedience that leads to every other sin. The Bible calls it the **fruit of deeds** (Micah 7:13).

"Those who plow iniquity and sow trouble reap the same" (Job 4:8).

"You have plowed wickedness . . . you have reaped iniquity. You have eaten the fruit of lies, because you have trusted in your own way" (Hosea 10:13).

"Do you not know that the unrighteous will not inherit the kingdom of God? Do not be deceived. Neither fornicators, nor idolaters, nor adulterers, nor homosexuals, nor sodomites, nor thieves, nor covetous, nor drunkards, nor revilers, nor extortioners will inherit the kingdom of God. And such were some of you" (1 Corinthians 6:9–11).

This is mankind's DNA, a hopeless profile if left only to human nature. But thank God He doesn't leave us to wallow in the forbidden wiles of worldliness. In Christ's death the Savior gives us new life. In man's despair God offers hope. In Satan's desire to devour us Jesus shows us the way of escape. And when the world persecutes believers, Jesus provides His sustaining grace. Because we are washed, we are sanctified, and we are justified in the name of the Lord Jesus and by the Spirit of our God. (1 Corinthians 6:11).

Possessing the fruits of the Spirit of God will . . .

Inject our hearts with love.

Infuse our experiences with joy.

Ingrain our motives with peace.

Increase our spirits through patience.

Impact our actions by kindness.

Illuminate our minds with goodness.

Inspire us to practice faithfulness.

Imprint our temperaments with gentleness.

Instill our desire to exhibit self-control.

The Bible tells us that our deeds produce fruit, good or bad. Through obedience to Jesus Christ, He will produce in us the fruit of His Spirit, which will then produce an abundant harvest of souls as others **"taste and see that the LORD is good" (Psalm 34:8).**

JESUS
IS LOVE

The fruit of the Spirit is love.

Galatians 5:22

When the seed of the Gospel takes root in our souls, it flourishes and produces a bountiful harvest known as the fruit of the Spirit. The Bible describes this fruit in Galatians 5. Our hearts can be injected with the spirit of love. When the Spirit of God takes up residence in our hearts, He sows the seeds of His attributes into the fertile soil of our thoughts, our speech, our attitudes, and our actions. This is part of His transforming power, and we must not resist the pruning He does to bring the fruit of His Spirit into every area of our lives. Scripture embodies the seed and fruit, planting and harvesting, weeding out wild briars, and gathering in sweetened kernels. Whether we realize it or not, these are things we are and things we do. We all sow seed through our actions—bad or good. We all bring forth

> We should all weed out the unlovely within and gather up the sweetness of Him.

fruit through our attitudes—rotten or sweet. We plant words in the minds of others with a hateful spirit or a loving heart. We all harvest thorns or blossoms that affect our thinking. We should all weed out the unlovely within and gather up the sweetness of Him.

The fruit of the Spirit of the living God is love. When Christ comes into our forgiven hearts, sin is removed, and the sweet sap of God's love fills the reservoir of our hearts. When a farmer harvests sap from a maple tree, he chisels a hole through the bark and into the tree trunk. He plunges into it a curved piece of wood or rubber, then attaches a bucket or rubber hose and allows the sap to run free into a catch basin. If the farmer is tapping multiple trees, large vats are standing ready to receive the sweet taste of the harvest. This is a picture of what Christ does in the lives of those who receive His seed of love. Through the greatest act of love ever demonstrated, Jesus hung—from splintered wood of His own creation—by nails thrust through His flesh. He was pierced by our sin and, in response, His precious blood was spilled out, covering the sins of all who are standing by, ready to receive the sweetness of this greatest attribute—*love*.

Do we exhibit sacrificial love that puts others before our own desires? Sowing this kind of love will turn the spade of dirt, exposing the seed of the Gospel to the nutrients of God's great love. But until we ourselves are sown with the love of God, the seed we sow will be wasted. The Lord says, "Indeed I am for you . . . and you shall be tilled and sown. I will multiply men upon you" (Ezekiel 36:9–10).

Do you fully trust God's love
to till the soil of your soul?

SOWING LOVE
IN A TIME OF LIES . . .

Morals and manners matter!

Political correctness (PC) has ruled the early days of the twenty-first century, causing people to go to extremes to soothe sensitivities, but it has led to a lack of sensibility. Many believe the better way is to just "tell it like it is," but often this is based on an individual's perception.

What we need to do is exhibit love by simply speaking the truth.

The truth is that morals and manners matter.

A worldly kind of love that is self-seeking will only ask, "What's in it for me?"

The fruit of the Spirit–kind of love is truth-seeking and asks, "What's in it that God can use?"

> *Love does not parade itself, is not puffed up; does not behave rudely, does not seek its own, is not provoked, thinks no evil; does not rejoice in iniquity, but rejoices in truth.*
>
> *1 Corinthians 13:4–6*

JESUS
IS JOY

The fruit of the Spirit is . . . joy.

Galatians 5:22

Our experiences can be infused with the spirit of joy. Many today interchange the words *joy* and *happiness*, but joy is something that has the ability to fill us even in the midst of unhappy circumstances. Joy is a condition of contentment. Jesus exemplified this in a way that challenges the human spirit. "Jesus . . . for the joy that was set before Him endured the cross" (Hebrews 12:2). Joy was the fruit of Christ's willingness to sacrificially bear our agony. He did it *joyfully* because He knew the end result—His death was going to bear everlasting fruit—the redeemed. "Behold, this is the joy of His way, and out of the earth others will grow" (Job 8:19).

True joy can only be found in the Lord Jesus Christ. He is the Source of joy—"that they may have My joy fulfilled in themselves" (John 17:13). Joy comes from His Word. "Your word was to me . . . joy" (Jeremiah 15:16). Joy is empowered by God's Spirit. "Now may the God of hope fill you with all joy and peace in believing . . . by the power of the Holy Spirit" (Romans 15:13).

The Bible assures us that when the seed of the Gospel takes root in the fertile soil of the heart, it will flourish with the fruit of joy—in times of trials, "You became followers . . . of the Lord, having received the word in much affliction, with joy of the Holy Spirit" (1 Thessalonians 1:6); in the midst of our work, "We . . . are fellow workers for your joy" (2 Corinthians 1:24); and as we grow older, "It is good and fitting . . . to enjoy the good of all his labor . . . all the days of his life which God gives him; for it is his heritage . . . this is the gift of God. . . . God keeps him busy with the joy of his heart" (Ecclesiastes 5:18–20).

> When the seed of the Gospel takes root in the fertile soil of the heart, it will flourish with the fruit of joy— in times of trials.

The Bible speaks of the "joy of faith" (Philippians 1:25); the "voice of joy" (Jeremiah 33:11); the "sound of joy" (Psalm 89:15); and the "joy of harvest" (Isaiah 9:3). The Bible tells us that we can ask for our joy to be full (John 16:24), and promises that no one will take our joy from us (John 16:22).

Are you sowing the Gospel seed in your sphere of influence with joy, anticipating a bountiful harvest?

SOWING JOY IN A TIME OF LIES . . .

People wear themselves out looking for happiness in all the wrong places. Sowing seeds of discontentment brings emptiness.

Busyness can be the devil's playground, distracting us from the important work of God—living for Him!

Distractions cause us to veer onto another pathway. Deception is taking the wrong way while believing we are still on the right road.

Worldly happiness is derived by the busyness of fun; it says, "Fulfill my desires."

The fruit of the Spirit–kind of joy is the ongoing state of contentment no matter the circumstances. True joy is fulfilling God's desires.

Godliness with contentment is great gain.

1 Timothy 6:6

JESUS
IS PEACE

The fruit of the Spirit is . . . peace.

Galatians 5:22

As the sower's seed grows and expands in our souls, our motives are ingrained with the spirit of peace. No one person meets the expectation of the Standard-Bearer, the Lord Jesus Christ. The world wants peace, so it claims; yet wars rage—proving that men are incapable of governing themselves. This is the reason Jesus came, to save men from themselves. His very name speaks of this fruit of the Spirit—He is the "God of peace" (Romans 15:33); the "king of peace" (Hebrews 7:2); the "Prince of Peace" (Isaiah 9:6). Who better to teach us the fruit of peace? "He . . . is our peace" (Ephesians 2:14), and He "has called us to peace" (1 Corinthians 7:15). Why then are we so often at odds with people, circumstances, society, and even ourselves? Perhaps it is because we don't embrace the Peacemaker—we don't believe and follow His example.

We are told in Scripture to "seek peace" (Psalm 34:14); to "love peace" (Zechariah 8:19); to "speak peace" (Zechariah 9:10 ESV); to "pursue peace" (Hebrews 12:14); to "be at peace" (1 Thessalonians 5:13); and to "go in peace" (Mark 5:34). The Bible tells us that peace is God's blessing (Psalm 29:11). He promised to give us "peace in believing" (Romans 15:13); peace of thought (Jeremiah 29:11); peace in sleep (Psalm 4:8); an "abundance of peace" (Psalm 37:11); "peace . . . within our walls" (Psalm 122:7); peace within our borders (Psalm 147:14); and "peace in heaven" (Luke 19:38).

Jesus proclaimed, "Blessed are the peacemakers" (Matthew 5:9); "Have peace one with another" (Mark 9:50); "Peace be still" (Mark 4:39); and often He greeted people with the phrase, "Peace to you" (Luke 24:36).

Is there any doubt that the Sower of the seed is also the Source of peace? "Peace I leave with you, My peace I give to you; not as the world gives" (John 14:27).

> The Bible instructs us to sow peace along our paths, one believer to another.

When peace is absent, we're looking at the world, not at Him. "God is not the author of confusion but of peace" (1 Corinthians 14:33). He brings us "the gospel of peace" (Romans 10:15), and He preached peace far and near (Ephesians 2:17). How is this peace attained? "We have peace with God through our Lord Jesus Christ" (Romans 5:1); it is multiplied through the knowledge of God (2 Peter 1:2) and "yields the peaceable fruit of righteousness" (Hebrews 12:11).

When we are obedient to Christ, He promises "to guide our feet into the way of peace" (Luke 1:79). "Great peace have those who love Your law, and nothing causes them to stumble" (Psalm 119:165). The Lord will also keep us in perfect peace when our minds are fixed on Him (Isaiah 26:3). He goes even further and says that "He will speak peace to His people" (Psalm 85:8), and will make even our enemies to be at peace with us (Proverbs 16:7).

As the Sower Himself has sown peace into our hearts, the Bible instructs us to sow peace along our paths, one believer to another (Romans 14:19), and to spread the "gospel of peace" to those who are "estranged from God" (Romans 10:15). "Now the fruit of righteousness is sown in peace by those who make peace" (James 3:18).

Are you exercising the God-given fruit of sowing peace along your way?

SOWING PEACE IN A TIME OF LIES . . .

The opposite of peace is conflict. Sowing seeds of despair leads to excusing bad behavior.

A worldly kind of peace is to coexist with no barriers, but this will only lead to chaos.

The fruit of the Spirit–kind of peace is honoring the boundaries God has designed for our good.

> *For they do not speak peace, but they devise deceitful matters against the quiet ones in the land. . . . Great peace have those who love Your law, and nothing causes them to stumble.*
>
> *Psalm 35:20; 119:165*

JESUS
IS LONGSUFFERING
(PATIENT)

The fruit of the Spirit is . . . longsuffering [patience].

Galatians 5:22

The fruit that springs forth from the good seed of the Gospel increases our spirits with patience. What comes to mind when you hear the word *patience*? Lost days of lingering? Dreadful delays? Passing the time? Waiting for an answer? The word *patience* actually speaks of strength, endurance, persistence, staying power, fortitude, vigor—a determined mind, a resilient will, a steadfast spirit, grit!

The patience of Job is an expression used even by the world. But many people may not realize that when they utter the phrase, they are actually quoting the Bible. Jesus' half brother James wrote, "Indeed we count them blessed who endure. You have heard of the *[patience] of Job* and seen the end intended by the Lord—that the Lord is very compassionate and merciful" (James 5:11). Job's legacy has stood the test of time, not because of his dreadful delay in hearing from God, or waiting on Him for an answer, or passing the time in the ash heap. Job's legacy lives on because of his grit. He exercised

> The word *patience* actually speaks of . . . a resilient will, a steadfast spirit, grit!

determination, resilience, and steadfastness in the midst of tragedy. How? Through patience—believing that God who was with him in good times would also be with him in bad times (Job 2:10).

This is the picture we see in the parable of the sower: "But the [seed] that fell on good ground are those who, having heard the word with a noble and good heart, keep it and bear fruit with patience" (Luke 8:15). While Job suffered every human heartache imaginable, he refused to curse God and die. Instead, he persevered. How can we possibly endure one tragedy after another without losing faith in God? The Bible says, "Whatever things were written before were written for our learning, that we through the patience and comfort of the Scriptures might have hope" (Romans 15:4). In the midst of deep suffering, Job said, "Though He slay me, yet will I trust Him" (Job 13:15). Job *patiently* trusted in God—he didn't let up. The Bible tells us that tribulation results in patience, experience, and hope (Romans 5:3–4). "No chastening seems to be joyful for the present, but painful; nevertheless, afterward it yields the peaceable fruit of righteousness to those who have been trained by it" (Hebrews 12:11).

First Timothy 6:11 tells us to run with patience, to "pursue patience," and we're told to "let patience have its perfect work" (James 1:4). None of this is possible without "the God of patience" (Romans 15:5). The Sower implants the seed, and the Holy Spirit produces fruit when we grow in the knowledge of God. The seed is nourished and grows into fruit-bearing *patience.*

"Here is the patience of the saints; here are those who keep the commandments of God and the faith of Jesus" (Revelation 14:12). "Walk worthy of the Lord, fully pleasing Him, being fruitful in every good work . . . for all patience and longsuffering with joy" (Colossians 1:10–11).

Are you seeing the fruit of patience being produced in your life, even when things aren't going your way?

SOWING PATIENCE
IN A TIME OF LIES . . .

Patience is often absent in a world that seeks immediate satisfaction. When mankind gets weary of waiting, it devises ways to make things happen; man's ways are restless and lack the virtue of patience.

The fruit of the Spirit's longsuffering is to demonstrate faith through prayer, maintaining confidence in the Lord as the Source of every good thing. His way is worth the wait.

But You, O Lord, are a God full of compassion, and gracious, longsuffering and abundant in mercy and truth.

Psalm 86:15

JESUS
IS KIND

The fruit of the Spirit is . . . kindness.

Galatians 5:22

Our actions impact others in a positive way when we exhibit the spirit of kindness, an attribute seriously lacking in our society today. No wonder. Our thoughts, many times, are far from the Lord Jesus, who exemplifies the meaning of this word. When Scripture speaks of the kindness of Christ, we see the compassion of Christ. When He saw the multitudes bringing the sick, He had compassion and healed them (Matthew 14:14). When He saw the crowds with nothing to eat, He had compassion and fed them (Matthew 15:32); when He saw the crowd like sheep without a shepherd, He had compassion on them and began to teach them many things (Mark 6:34).

> Jesus' kindness was so pure that the Bible writers used many adjectives to convey this Christlike attribute.

The fruit of kindness that the Lord exhibited is compelling. Jesus' kindness was so pure that the Bible writers used many adjectives to convey this Christlike attribute. The Lord displayed His "*marvelous* kindness" (Psalm 31:21); His "*merciful* kindness" (Psalm 117:2); His "*everlasting* kindness" (Isaiah 54:8); His "*great* kindness" (Joel 2:13); and the "*exceeding riches* . . . in His kindness" (Ephesians 2:7). Every kind word He spoke, every kind act He did, every kind step He took paved the way to the cross, where the *most marvelous, great,* and *merciful* kindness toward mankind was offered to the lost world. "But when the kindness . . . of God our Savior toward man appeared . . . He saved us" (Titus 3:4–5). The Lord is our example, and this is why we are told to "put on . . . kindness" (Colossians 3:12).

When our heart produces the rotten fruit of harshness instead of graciousness, spitefulness instead of thoughtfulness, or maliciousness instead of gentleness, we are assisting Satan in his acts of cruelty against God's creation. The Bible says, "We are to God the fragrance of Christ among those who are being saved and among those who are perishing" (2 Corinthians 2:15). Are we living up to this marvelous standard?

Is your heart producing
rotten fruit or the sweet-smelling
savor of kindness?

SOWING KINDNESS IN
A TIME OF LIES . . .

People cry out for justice according to their way while refusing to admit their guilt.

True kindness is the absence of hostility, and produces a gracious spirit. When the seed of kindness is sown, it can cause even our enemies to retreat.

Beware of the charms along the journey. Take hold of the virtues that guide your steps.

> *What is desired in a man is kindness, and a poor man is better than a liar.*
>
> *Proverbs 19:22*

JESUS
IS GOOD

The fruit of the Spirit is . . . goodness.

Galatians 5:23

When God's attributes are planted within, our minds are illuminated with the spirit of goodness. The Bible says that no one is good, "No, not one" (Romans 3:10). So then, how are we to possess the fruit of goodness? The answer comes from the Spirit of God—it is His fruit of goodness, not ours. "The fruit of the Spirit is in all goodness, righteousness, and truth" (Ephesians 5:9). Lest we think ourselves good, Romans 3 tells us that we are all sinners and possess no good thing. Thankfully, the Bible later tells us, "Having been set free from sin . . . you have your fruit to holiness, and the end, everlasting life" (Romans 6:22). We were dead in sin but are now alive in Christ. The redeemed sinner is to *put on* Christ. We must speak His language, convey His heart, think His thoughts, walk in His footsteps, and wear His light. This is how we obey God's Word.

> We must speak His language, convey His heart, think His thoughts, walk in His footsteps, and wear His light.

The redeemed are no longer seen by God as sinners. He sees those who are saved through His Son, Jesus Christ. That's why His Spirit can impart *goodness*. "Is the Spirit of the LORD restricted? Are these His doings? Do not My words do *good* to him who walks uprightly?" (Micah 2:7). "For God gives wisdom and knowledge and joy to a man who is good in His sight" (Ecclesiastes 2:26).

Jesus said, "I have called you friends, for all things that I heard from My Father I have made known to you. . . . You should go and bear fruit" (John 15:15–16). Those of us who have received the Sower's seed will bear the fruit of the Spirit. Our moment-by-moment prayer should be, "Teach me to do Your will, for You are my God; Your Spirit is good" (Psalm 143:10). This is the only way we can possess *goodness*. When we receive Christ, He comes into our lives and we are partakers of His attributes. While many want to believe that God's riches mean gold and silver, His riches (the attributes of Himself) are far more bountiful and precious than man's idea of wealth (Proverbs 16:16). "The wisdom that is from above is first pure, then peaceable, gentle, willing to yield, full of mercy and *good* fruits" (James 3:17).

Willing to yield is an interesting phrase. When we are filled with God's Spirit, we have willingly surrendered what we possess—rotten fruit—for God's fruit, exchanging our evil for His *goodness.*

"And God is able to make all grace abound toward you, that you, always having all sufficiency in all things, may have an abundance for every *good* work" (2 Corinthians 9:8). "Walk worthy of the Lord, fully pleasing Him, being fruitful in every *good* work" (Colossians 1:10), and be "filled with the fruits of righteousness [goodness]" (Philippians 1:11). The psalmist declared, "Oh, taste and see that the LORD is good" (Psalm 34:8).

Will you pray daily that the Lord will infuse you with the fruit of goodness as you flourish in Him?

SOWING GOODNESS IN A TIME OF LIES . . .

Some people love the "gotcha moment." So does Satan. Those who slander and express malice toward others are a sure sign of the devil's handiwork. He strokes the ego, leading people to diminish others to make themselves look good. Watch out! Satan's "gotcha" where he wants you. Anything that distracts from the Lord Jesus is the work of the devil.

Sowing seeds of God's good and righteous attributes will keep our feet on the ground and our eyes on the Lord. When we diminish our own self-importance, His Spirit increases our ability to exhibit the goodness of His grace toward others.

Do not remember the sins . . . nor my transgressions; according to Your mercy remember me, for Your goodness' sake, O LORD. . . . I would have lost heart, unless I had believed that I would see the goodness of the LORD in the land of the living.

Psalm 25:7; 27:13

JESUS
IS FAITHFUL

The fruit of the Spirit is . . . faithfulness.

Galatians 5:22

God's Spirit inspires us to practice faithfulness. Most of us think we exhibit faithfulness simply by expressing faith in the Lord Jesus Christ. Yet faithfulness is more than just breathing a word of testimony. Picture faithfulness as a fruit that, when broken open, exposes multiple seeds that have the potential of reproducing more of the same fruit if sown, or planted, in rich soil.

These seeds inside the fruit of faithfulness can be described as reliable, trustworthy, dependable, true, dedicated, accurate—believable. This is a word picture of the Lord Jesus—the One who embodies all of these attributes. He imparts these to us when He sows the Gospel seed into our lives and forgives us for our sinful fruit of faith*less*ness. The Bible says, "If we confess our sins, He is faithful and just to forgive us our sins, and to cleanse us from all unrighteousness" (1 John 1:9). It is because of His faithfulness that we can become men and women who are trustworthy servants of God, dependable spouses and children, dedicated worshipers, reliable employees, dependable employers, true friends, and believable witnesses.

> Faithfulness is more than just breathing a word of testimony.

The Lord Jesus increases our abilities by endowing us with His own virtues. "Grace and peace be multiplied to you . . . as His divine power has given to us all things that pertain to life and godliness . . . who called us by glory and virtue" (2 Peter 1:2–3). It is interesting to read these words from probably the roughest disciple of them all: the one who overreacted, spoke out of turn, and then turned around and did exactly what he said he would not do. Peter said he would be faithful to Jesus, and before he knew it, he denied the Lord and ran. Here we see a disciple who had grown from the milk of the Word, to the meat of the Word, and finally to the fruit of the Word. When Peter began to feed on the loveliness of the Lord Jesus, he grew strong in his faith and he became faithful. Jesus had sown a powerful seed in some shallow soil, but it took root. Then Peter passed on what the Lord passed on to him, telling others to add to their faith virtue, knowledge, self-control, perseverance, godliness, kindness, and love—the fruit of the Spirit. "For if these things are yours and abound," Peter writes, "you will be neither barren nor unfruitful" (2 Peter 1:5–8) as you live for Christ.

The Bible tells us that "God is faithful" (1 Corinthians 1:9) and the "faithful Creator" (1 Peter 4:19). He is faithful "every night" (Psalm 92:2); His counsel is faithful (Isaiah 25:1); His testimonies are faithful (Psalm 119:138); and His commandments are faithful (Psalm 119:86). We are told that Jesus Christ is the "faithful witness" (Revelation 1:5), and His name is "Faithful and True" (Revelation 19:11).

Because He has declared His faithfulness to man (Psalm 40:10), the Bible declares that man should also "be found faithful" (1 Corinthians 4:2). Jesus Christ promised to preserve the faithful, for "He who calls you is faithful" (1 Thessalonians 5:24). How does this happen? We become faithful as we hold fast to His faithful Word (Titus 1:9) and speak His Word faithfully (Jeremiah 23:28), for a faithful witness will not lie (Proverbs 14:5), but speak the truth—God's truth.

When the skin of your fruit
is peeled back, will what is inside
your heart be found faithful?

SOWING FAITHFULNESS IN A TIME OF LIES . . .

Faithfulness is foreign to those who continually speak dishonest words, who are fraudulent in their thinking, and who are corrupt in their actions. Such a life exhibits the rotten fruit of faithlessness.

Those who grow weary can find redemption in Christ, the faithful One, who will rescue our souls from the chokehold of the world.

> *There is no faithfulness in their mouth; their inward part is destruction; their throat is an open tomb; they flatter with their tongue . . . [they] fall by their own counsels. . . . Trust in the LORD, and do good; dwell in the land, and feed on His faithfulness.*
>
> *Psalm 5:9–10; 37:3*

JESUS
IS GENTLE

The fruit of the Spirit is . . . gentleness.

Galatians 5:23

Our temperaments can leave imprints of gentleness. "A servant of the Lord must be . . . gentle to all" (2 Timothy 2:24). This is what Paul wrote to Timothy. Paul told Titus to remind followers of Christ to be prepared "for every good work," to speak evil of no man, and to be "gentle, showing all humility to all men" (Titus 3:1–2). Many times we overlook words in Scripture that seem insignificant. But here we see *all* mentioned twice: "showing *all* humility to *all* men." Naturally no one person ever comes in contact with "all" people, but this little word urges us to show complete humility toward everyone we come in contact with.

Timothy and Titus were Paul's spiritual sons, young men who had been saved under Paul's ministry. They bore fruit from the seed that Paul sowed while preaching the Word of God. These young pastors had their share of struggles, but Paul continued sowing truth into their lives, instructing, correcting, and encouraging them in the faith and in their leadership. Timothy and Titus encountered a great number of people from different backgrounds and persuasions. Paul emphasized the importance of being gentle, but then he described those who lack the gentle fruit of the Spirit and have no apparent interest in knowing Christ. "Avoid foolish disputes . . . contentions, and strivings about the law; for they are unprofitable and useless. Reject a divisive man after the first and second admonition, knowing that such a person is warped and sinning" (Titus 3:9–11).

You may feel that rejecting someone is not such a gentle approach, but nowhere in Scripture does the Lord instruct His followers to overlook, excuse, or accept another way other than God's way. This is why Jesus came: to show mankind "the way" (John 14:6). Subjecting ourselves to disputes, contentions, and strivings is not the way of following the gentle Savior. Paul pleaded with the Corinthians, warning them of false teachers in the church, but he pleaded with "the meekness and gentleness of Christ" (2 Corinthians 10:1). "Who is wise and understanding among you? Let him show by good conduct that his works are done

> Nowhere in Scripture does the Lord instruct His followers to overlook, excuse, or accept another way other than God's way.

in the meekness of wisdom . . . if you have . . . self-seeking in your hearts . . . this wisdom does not descend from above, but is earthly, sensual, demonic . . . but the wisdom that is from above is . . . gentle" (James 3:13–17).

> Are you willing to show complete humility toward others as they observe the fruit of your gentle spirit?

SOWING GENTLENESS IN A TIME OF LIES . . .

Maligning gentleness as a weakness is godless. A gentle spirit is the mark of humbleness, exemplified by Jesus leaving heaven's glory to live in a sin-ridden world.

Humility is not for the weak but for the strong. Those who seek a humble and gentle temperament are often used by God to quiet the storm.

If anyone . . . does not consent to wholesome words, even the words of our Lord Jesus Christ . . . he is proud, knowing nothing, but is obsessed with disputes . . . and destitute of the truth. . . . But you, O man of God, flee these things and pursue righteousness . . . [and] gentleness. . . . There is one whose rash words are like sword thrusts, but the tongue of the wise brings healing.

1 Timothy 6:3–5, 11; Proverbs 12:18 ESV

JESUS
IS SELF-CONTROLLED
(DISCIPLINED)

The fruit of the Spirit is . . . self-control.

Galatians 5:23

Walking in step with the Lord leads us to an increasing desire to please God. The world has immersed itself with self-image, self-identity, self-esteem, and self-improvement. All of this creates a veneer of excessive self-promotion by gratifying every whim of appetite and desire.

If we are going to be indulgent, let's be extravagantly indulgent for the One who has given us life and the will to live it for His glory. For Christians who seek after the things of Christ, they are not consumed with satisfying their flesh, which leads to corruption. The Bible tells us to sow to the Spirit and reap life everlasting (Galatians 6:8). We struggle with this in our mortal bodies, but God in His Word promises to help us when we are tempted and wrestling with the things of the world.

Jesus was an example to us in earthly form. Jesus "made Himself of no reputation, taking the form of a bondservant, and coming in the likeness of men. . . . He humbled Himself" (Philippians 2:7–8). Since He is the One we look to as the pattern for living, we are to "let nothing be done through selfish ambition or conceit. . . . Let each of you look out not only for his own interests, but also for the interests of others" (Philippians

2:3–4). Paul tells us to "have no confidence in the flesh" (Philippians 3:3). Then he paints a word picture of the fruit of the Spirit that enables us to exercise restraint (self-control): Whatever things are true, noble, just, pure, lovely, of good report—if there is anything virtuous or worthy of praise—think on these things (Philippians 4:8).

Jesus is the source and example of self-control. When He cleanses our corrupt flesh and robes us in His righteousness, we become God-controlled—stepping out of self-indulgence into God-indulgence. We're not consumed with self-image because we know we are made in God's image (Genesis 1:26). We are not steeped in self-identification because we're identified with Christ: "That the life of Jesus also may be manifested in our body . . . that the life of Jesus

> We're not consumed with self-image because we know we are made in God's image.

also may be manifested in our mortal flesh . . . since we have the same spirit of faith" (2 Corinthians 4:10–13). We don't have to clamor for glamour and self-esteem; instead, "in lowliness of mind let each esteem others better than himself" (Philippians 2:3). We don't have to constantly be running to self-improvement classes; we have been transformed by Christ (Romans 12:2). We don't have to undergo cosmetic alterations. Jesus Christ gives us a makeover the moment we step into His glorious forgiveness and newness of life. When He sends us out into the world, He has made us over by the fruit of His Spirit, with the command to go forth and sow seed that will produce an abundant harvest.

There is nothing more appetizing than to walk into a farmers' market and behold the appetizing, multi-colored fruit overflowing in the baskets. Is this what our lives reflect? Does the world peer into our lives and see the gathering of bountiful fruit colored crimson that speaks of Christ's sacrificial love, and the luscious yellow fruit as bright as God's eternal Light?

Has the Sower's seed in your life produced fruit so evident that it would cause others to taste and see that the Lord is good in all of His benefits?

SOWING DISCIPLINE IN
A TIME OF LIES . . .

Man's condemnation shows no restraint. Man's judgment, when not guided by God's righteousness, is undisciplined and leads to rebellion.

Whatever we take control of usually ends up controlling us!

We exhibit self-control when we take our hands off of our lives and circumstances and turn the controls over to God. Independence is when we choose to let God master us.

> *There is therefore now no condemnation to those who are in Christ Jesus, who do not walk according to the flesh, but according to the Spirit. . . . Those who walk according to the flesh . . . are presumptuous, self-willed. . . . For all that is in the world . . . the pride of life—is not of the Father but is of the world.*
>
> *Romans 8:1; 2 Peter 2:10; 1 John 2:16*

JESUS, THE PARABLE OF THE SOWER, SEED, AND THE SOIL

I am the true vine, and My Father is the vinedresser. Every branch in Me that does not bear fruit He takes away; and every branch that bears fruit He prunes, that it may bear more fruit.

John 15:1-2

Lord, may the parable You spoke centuries ago

Spring forth with new life as Your Word is made
    known

May the seed of the Gospel find fertile ground

In the hearts of the lost the whole world around

If the seed is not buried in the soil of the heart

No life will take root and hope will depart

The winds of adversity will sweep it away

To the rocks and the briars and there it will lay

The birds will snatch seed and take to the air

Leaving the soul in the darkest despair

Some seed will settle in dry, stony soil

Seared by the sun where roots cannot toil

May the seed not be carried by the doctrine of men

That lay among weeds where hearts do not bend

Or fall by the wayside where shallow it hides

Among the thorns and thistles that bind

May sowers handle the seed of Your Word

Planting it deep so Your Spirit is heard

Let the tears of many water through prayer

The seed of Your Gospel You've given to share.

Do you know the Sower of the seed?

Rejoice in Him.

Has the seed been planted in the soil of your heart?

Receive from Him.

Are you a branch that is being nourished by the True Vine?

Remain in Him.

—_Donna Lee Toney_

ABOUT THE AUTHORS

Franklin Graham, the eldest son of Billy and Ruth Graham, serves as president and CEO of Samaritan's Purse and the Billy Graham Evangelistic Association, and is a best-selling author. He has traveled the world meeting the needs of poor, sick, and suffering people in more than 100 countries. As an evangelist he has led crusades around the world. He and his wife, Jane Austin, live in Boone, North Carolina, and have four children and several grandchildren.

Donna Lee Toney has been a colleague of Franklin Graham's for thirty-five years and has been involved in the ministries of Samaritan's Purse and the Billy Graham Evangelistic Association and in literary collaboration with the Grahams since 1982. Most recently, she has co-authored *Operation Christmas Child: A Story of Simple Gifts* with Franklin Graham, and recently released titles by Billy Graham: *Where I Am* and *The Reason for My Hope*.